THE WOKE REVOLUTION

The WOKE REVOLUTION

UP FROM SLAVERY AND BACK AGAIN

H.V. TRAYWICK, JR.

SHOTWELL

COLUMBIA · So. CAR.

EST. 2015

PUBLISHING

Produced in the Republic of South Carolina by
SHOTWELL PUBLISHING LLC
Post Office Box 2592
Columbia, So. Carolina 29202
www.ShotwellPublishing.com

Cover: Design by Boo Jackson. Photo by H.V. Traywick, Jr.

ISBN: 978-1-963506-47-1

FIRST EDITION

10 9 8 7 6 5 4 3 2 1

Dedicated to the Memory of

Edmund Ruffin

Planter, Soil Scientist, and Old Virginia Fire-Eater.

I stood in the rain, far from home at nightfall

By the Potomac, the great Dome lit the water,

The city my blood had built I knew no more

While the screech-owl whistled his new delight

Consecutively dark...

—Allen Tate, *Aneas at Washington*[1]

Contents

The M/V Stella Nova

IN EARLY 1971, I was sailing in the engine room of a little coastal tramp of Bermudan registry laden with a cargo of twine from Haiti, and bound for New London, Connecticut. One night during the mid-watch, after checking the bilges and the gauges, I went up to the galley to refill my coffee cup. Upon turning on the light, I had a momentary sense of the bulkheads being alive as in a nightmare, until I realized that they were crawling with carpets of cockroaches which had infested the ship from the cargo of twine. But with the sudden shock of the light, they disappeared into the shadows and crevasses without a trace, and all appeared as before.

In the summer of 2020, with the death and apotheosis of George Floyd, the Woke Revolution broke forth in virtue-posting riots, looting, arson, vandalism, iconoclasm, and the destruction of urban businesses all across the United States. ANTIFA and Black Lives Matter mobs filled the streets with hurled brickbats, frozen water bottles, and zip-loc bags of excrement in this so-called "mostly peaceful summer of love," fulfilling in America the role of Chairman Mao's Communist Red Guards. The pandering "woke" administration then carried on its "Long March" of Cultural Revolution with its totalitarian mandates concerning the manufactured Wuhan virus and the Covid 19 pandemic, the defunding of police, FBI raids on political opponents, "lawfare" by rogue prosecutors, "enabled" assassination attempts, open borders, government indoctrination in schools at all levels, widespread suppression of free speech, and widespread destruction of traditions, until the shock of the November 2024 election gave them pause. At this writing it is uncertain whether the present administration will take to the shadows, or be wielding its "lame duck" powers for more mischief before the new administration takes office in January, but in any case, like the Motor Vessel *Stella Nova*, the United States remain infested with cockroaches.

H.V. Traywick, Jr.
Richmond, Virginia
November 2024

Introduction

The Woke Revolution

"Live asses will kick at dead lions..."
—Admiral Raphael Semmes, CSN[2]

ADMIRAL RAPHAEL SEMMES, late of the Confederate Navy, and late commander of the famous commerce raider CSS *Alabama*, told of our origins:

> "The American Republic, as has been said, was a failure, because of the antagonism of the two peoples attempted to be bound together in the same government... The dissimilarity between the people of the Northern, and the people of the Southern States has always been remarked upon by observant foreigners, and it has not escaped the attention of our own historians. Indeed, it could not be otherwise, for the origin of the two sections has been diverse. Virginia and Massachusetts were the two original germs from which the great majority of the American population has sprung; and no two peoples, speaking the same language and coming from the same country, could have been more dissimilar in education, taste, and habits, and even in natural instincts, than were the adventurers who settled these two colonies. Those who sought a new field of adventure for themselves, and affluence for their posterity, in the

more congenial climate of the Chesapeake, were the gay, and dashing cavaliers, who, as a class, afterward adhered to the fortunes of the Charleses, whilst the first settlers of Massachusetts were composed of the same materials that formed the 'Praise-God-Bare-bones' Parliament of Cromwell.

"These two peoples seem to have had an instinctive repugnance, the one to the other. To use a botanical phrase, the Puritan was a seedling of the English race which had been unknown to it before. It had few, or none of the characteristics of the original stock. Gloomy, saturnine, and fanatical in disposition, it seemed to repel all the more kindly and generous impulses of our nature, and to take pleasure in pulling down everything that other men had built up; not so much, as its subsequent history would seem to show, because the work was faulty, as because it had been done by other hands than their own. They hated tyranny, for instance, but it was only because they were not themselves the tyrants..."[3]

Their military victory at Appomattox in 1865, and their subsequent arbitrary political power during Reconstruction, set them on their "Long March" towards the fulfillment of their ambitions for a totalitarian government under their control. Their Puritan hatred of the South was in full flower during the 2020 "summer of love" with the vandalizing and destruction of Confederate war memorials all across the South. As Tennyson wrote,

Yea, they would pare the mountain to the plain

To leave an equal baseness...[4]

Thomas Carlyle said that it takes men of worth to recognize worth in men.[5] Among the many worthy men across Western Civilization who recognized the worth of General Robert E. Lee was Sir Winston Churchill, who summed it up by saying that Lee was one of the noblest Americans who ever lived and one of the greatest captains in the annals of war.[6] But the Lee Monument in Richmond was vandalized and desecrated by mobs of rioting "wokelings," and taken down by the groveling scalawag Governor Ralph Northam, who, loving his office more than his honor, said that Lee no longer represented the values of Virginia. Judging by the filthy graffiti that desecrated the Lee Monument, before it was taken down to the cheers of the mob, I would say no truer words have ever been spoken. What remained was an empty traffic circle full of trash and drug paraphernalia as a monument to the moral depravity of this Age without a Name.

We are in a Marxist revolution rife with Puritan overtones. Critical Race Theory merely replaces traditional Marxist class warfare with race warfare, with White people—and particularly Southern White people and the conveniently long-dead Confederacy—designated as scapegoats for all the racial ills in the Yankee Empire, and apostates deserving the fate of Salem witches in John Winthrop's Puritan "City upon a hill."

Ever since the Spring of 1864, Southerners have been on the defensive. No war was ever won on the defensive, but we have spent barrels of ink explaining the righteousness of our Cause, often mistakenly confounding the many causes of secession with the single cause of the war, which was *secession itself. That* is what the war was "about," and what we were fighting for was simply our independence from those who would deny it, *just as in 1776, when the thirteen (slave-holding)[7] Colonies seceded from the British Empire.* But rather than hammering our detractors with this simple Truth, we instead get ourselves into involved defensive explanations that cause their eyes to glaze over, and when "the defense rests," they calmly look at us and say "Slavery." It is a political axiom that whenever your opponent gets you to explain, you have already lost the argument. Therefore, it is better to take the offensive rather than the defensive, fix bayonets, and indict the hypocrisy of our detractors and their *Myth of the Righteous Cause.* The agitation over our Confederate monuments rests upon this fossilized myth, which proclaims that "The Civil War was all about slavery, the righteous North waged it to free the slaves, and the evil South fought to keep them. End of story. Any questions?"

Well, yes. First, to claim that the South went to war to keep their slaves, one must also claim that the North went to war to free them. The simple fact is that it did not. Abraham Lincoln boldly admitted that fact in his First Inaugural.[8] So, the first question to them is, do they expect us to doubt the word of "Honest Abe"? The next question is, if the North went to war to free the slaves, why was slavery constitutional in the United States throughout the entire war? When some of the Northern States abolished slavery for its inutility in their industrializing society, they did not free their slaves. Instead, they sold them South before their abolition laws went into effect.[9] But there still were "slave States" in the Union throughout the war, so if the righteous North went to war to free slaves, as the *Myth of the Righteous Cause* has it, why didn't they free their own? And why did Abraham Lincoln's *Emancipation Proclamation*—issued halfway through the war when the South was winning it—say that slavery was all right as long as one were loyal to his government?[10] And why did Lincoln—a documented White Supremacist who tried until the day he died to deport the Black race in the United States back to Africa[11]—choose to inaugurate the bloodiest war in the history of the Western Hemisphere to, in effect, drive Southern slavery and four million Southern Blacks back *into* the Union, when he could have well been rid of them all without firing a shot? Do the grammar school histories indoctrinating our children or the Marxist professors of our higher education schools, colleges and universities say anything about all this bald-faced hypocrisy of the self-righteous North?

In his Second Inaugural, Lincoln claimed that the South was fighting to expand slavery into the Territories.[12] That was certainly a political issue before the war, but with the South out of the Union, the Confederacy had given up all claims to the United States Territories, making Lincoln's specious claim just one more smelly "red herring" to cover the tracks of his murderous usurpation of power in waging his war of invasion, conquest, and coerced political allegiance against the South. But since Lincoln did not recognize the Southern States as being out of the Union,[13] by his own definition he was committing treason under Article III, section 3 of the Constitution by waging war against them. Lincoln was the usurper and the traitor, not Jefferson Davis. Nowhere does the Constitution prohibit self-defense. Secession is merely freedom of association writ large. There were many causes of secession, not least of which that Southerners no longer wished to be associated with those people who slandered, despised, and hated them to the point of not only wishing to see them swept from the face of the earth in a replay of the savage horrors of the St. Domingue slave insurrection, but of trying to instigate such horrors by financing John Brown's actual attempt at Harper's Ferry. But that begs the question of why those people waged the war to prevent their departure. To hear their vitriol, one would think they would have been glad to be rid of these Southern Apostates polluting what the New England Pilgrim Fathers called their "City upon a hill." But they weren't, for running like a river beneath their bigoted pieties was their avariciousness. Follow the dollar and know the truth. Quite simply, cotton was "king" in 1861, and the South's "Cotton Kingdom" was the North's "cash cow." With the South out of the Union free trading with Europe, and with the South in control of the mouth of the Mississippi River which drained the heartland, the North's "Mercantile Kingdom" would collapse from the colossal loss of trade and tariffs, and of cotton for her mills![14] So, Lincoln rebuffed every Southern overture for peace and launched an armada against Charleston Harbor to provoke South Carolina into firing the first shot.[15] South Carolina responded to Lincoln's provocation just as Massachusetts—the self-anointed "Patriot State"—had responded to George III's provocation at Lexington and Concord in 1775. Lincoln got the war he wanted in order to "save the Union" (for Northern interests), but it put him into the shoes of George III. As Tocqueville observed in his classic *Democracy in America*, "If the Union were to undertake to enforce by arms the allegiance of the confederate States by military means, it would be in a position very analogous to that of England at the time of the War of Independence."[16]

Virginia, "The Mother of States and of Statesmen," stood solidly for the Union she had done so much to create, but when Lincoln called for her troops to subjugate the Southern States, Virginia refused, indicted Lincoln for "choosing to inaugurate civil war,"[17] seceded from the Union, and joined the Confederacy. Four other States—including occupied Missouri—followed her out. But after four years of arduous service, as General Lee said at Appomattox, the South was compelled to yield to overwhelming numbers and resources,[18] and Lincoln drove the Southern States back into the Union at the point of the bayonet. Although John Wilkes Booth made a martyr out of America's Caesar, Reconstruction cemented his conquest. With an Army of Occupation and the pretense of law, and with the Union League stirring up racial hatred and putting the South under Negro rule for the sake of Radical Republican votes, a corrupt Northern political party destroyed the voluntary Union of sovereign States and "Reconstructed" it into a coerced Yankee Empire pinned together by bayonets.

The conquered Southern States, accepting the situation at the behest of General Lee, sent their representatives to Congress in December of 1865, but they were not allowed to take their seats. Vindictive Thaddeus Stevens of Pennsylvania stated: "The future condition of the conquered power depends on the will of the conqueror. They must come in as new States or remain as conquered provinces. Congress ... is the only power that can act in the matter... Congress must create States and declare when they are entitled to be represented... As there are no symptoms that the people of these provinces will be prepared to participate in constitutional government for some years, I know of no arrangement so proper for them as territorial governments. There they can learn the principles of freedom and eat the fruit of foul rebellion..."—a blatant case of Projection if there ever was one.[19]

In that session, the Thirteenth Amendment, abolishing slavery in the United States, was proposed, sent to the States, and ratified. This freed the slaves in the North—three years after Lincoln's *Emancipation Proclamation*. The Fourteenth Amendment was then proposed. It barred all ex-Confederates from Federal and State offices, and it required the Southern States to share in the payment of the Union war debt and repudiate their own. Tennessee ratified, but the ten ex-Confederate States that rejected it lost their identities in March of 1867 with the passage by Congress of the First Reconstruction Act, which cemented Radical Republican control of the government and turned the once-sovereign States into its provinces.[20]

The Reconstruction Act of 1867 put the ten Southern States under martial law and divided them into five military districts, with Virginia being designated as "Military District Number One." It enfranchised Southern Blacks (but not Northern Blacks), and stipulated that each Southern State frame a new constitution that met with Yankee approval. This was to be done by a convention consisting of male delegates "of whatever race, color, or previous condition"—with the exception of all ex-Confederate soldiers and most other Southern White men, all of whom were disfranchised for "participating in the rebellion." Then, when the new legislature elected under this new constitution had ratified the proposed Fourteenth Amendment, that State would be "readmitted into the Union" with representation in Congress. But if these States were *out* of the Union and under martial law, how could they ratify an amendment to the Constitution? And if they were *in* the Union, how could they be compelled to ratify it? The answer, of course, is Federal bayonets. Reconstruction was as much a calculated revolution as the Bolshevik Revolution of 1917, freeing slaves, then enslaving free men to a totalitarian government—a government entirely in the hands of the North.

Results? For the North? "The Gilded Age." For the South? Grinding poverty in a land laid waste until the Second World War, and the curse of being ruled by little men. For the Blacks? A recent study of military and Freedman's Bureau records has revealed that between 1862 and 1870 perhaps as many as *a million ex-slaves*, or *twenty-five percent of the population*, died of starvation, disease, and neglect under their Northern "liberators"![21] *This was more than the total number of Union and Confederate soldiers killed in the war combined.* Freed from their master's care, "Father Abraham, The Great Emancipator," had told them to "root hog, or die." The enfranchisement of Blacks in the South (but not in the North until the ratification of Amendment XV in 1870) was not due to any Northern altruism, as *The Myth of the Righteous Cause* would have us believe. It was merely a cynical Northern political tool to make the Southern States reliably Republican and to cement the North's conquest with their electoral votes. Once she had achieved it with her so-called "Reconstruction," the North abandoned her Black puppets to the upheaval she had wrought in Southern society and turned her attention to the Plains Indians, who were in the way of her trans-continental railroads. But that's another story— let the Indians tell you that one.

The gradual reconciliation after Reconstruction came in part from the South's "acceptance of the situation," and in part from the North's recognition of the South's difficulty in trying to assimilate millions of half-civilized Africans into Western Civilization. Since the North had gotten all she wanted—which was unfettered control of the Federal Government—she was content to let the South deal with that problem. However, when Southern Blacks started moving North to the Promised Land, they found themselves relegated by a cold Northern racism into segregated ghettos, and discovered that the Northern rhetoric about social equality was a political sham. The invention of television gave Northern politicians a way out of this embarrassing situation by giving them the means to divert Black attention from *de facto* Northern segregation onto the *de jure* segregation in the South, but their demagoguery provoked race riots up North. Desperate, guilt-ridden Northern White Liberals were driven to devise new crusades to divert the attention of their unwanted Black population onto Southern scapegoats. First came the invasion of the "Freedom Riders"—locked arm-in-arm with Black marchers down South—protesting Southern segregation and posting their Progressive virtues before the TV cameras for all to see. But while they were delivering tutorials on proper race relations to the benighted Southerners, the Blacks up North were burning their cities down—and they have been doing so ever since, forever compelling Desperate White Liberals to devise new crusades upon which to post their virtues.

Their latest crusade—integral with the "Woke Revolution"—is not only the destruction and removal of Confederate Monuments, but the obliteration from memory of all vestiges of the Confederacy. But when all of the Confederate monuments have been vandalized and torn down and all the streets, schools and military bases have been renamed, what will their next targets be? Be assured that these self-righteous, Latter-Day Puritans will not rest, for crusading, witch-burning and virtue posting are in their DNA. It came over in the *Mayflower*. Meanwhile, Monument Avenue in Richmond is a desecrated shambles; Thomas Jefferson is under assault at UVA; W&L has repudiated General Lee; and VMI has repudiated "Stonewall" Jackson, while her Cadets who fought and died at the Battle of New Market and are buried at VMI have become an embarrassment (and a rebuke) to the administration! But not to worry—when all Confederate monuments in the South have been torn down, peace, love, and diversity will flow like a river from Minneapolis and Seattle to Chicago and Philadelphia, and Desperate White Liberal Crusaders will be anointing themselves before the TV cameras all across the Yankee Empire.

Meanwhile, as the "woke" mania for the destruction of every tradition and every foundation of civilization and culture—in defiance of science, biology and nature—and the replacement of these with Equity for every conceivable definition of race, gender, and species reaches beyond the point of absurdity in the Victimhood Olympics, we have been carried away into Babylon, with women being sent into combat while men push baby buggies around town; with the government funding infanticide and sex-change operations while girls become Boy Scouts and men "choose" to be women; with children "deciding" their gender and being given access to the bathroom of their choice in school, while anarchy rules the classrooms and teachers are being assaulted by their students without redress; with government schools turned into neo-Marxist indoctrination centers where Critical Race Theory is taught as history and transgenderism is promoted as the norm, while conservative speakers at colleges are being hounded off campus by ANTIFA and Black Lives Matter mobs; with race-norming instead of merit and SAT scores determining college admissions, while grading in classwork is being abolished as "racist" when Blacks fail to meet the standards; with laws being made to conform to barbaric behavior instead of barbaric behavior being made to conform to the law, while convicts are being paroled into society to create racial parity in prisons and the defunded and demonized police are throwing down their badges in disgust; with the National debt approaching thirty six trillion dollars and the U.S. Government running riot with it like a teenager with a bottle of whiskey and his daddy's car keys, while inflation runs rampant and the homeless are begging on every street corner for the increasingly more worthless dollar; with a totalitarian government bankrupting businesses and threatening free citizens with draconian penalties if they don't take the Covid-19 vaccine and wear a mask in public, while the Third World is swarming across the open borders unchecked and unvaccinated... As one commentator said recently, we have become so open-minded that our brains have fallen out.

This may appear to be the height of insanity, but it is not. This is all evil political calculation. If Reconstruction was calculated like the Communist Bolshevik Revolution in Russia in 1917 to give political control of the country to the revolutionaries, today's "Woke Revolution" is fanaticism like the French Revolution's bloody Reign of Terror, and calculated to destroy Western Civilization root and branch in order to build up a New World Order. Perhaps the Confederate monuments will be replaced by the guillotine.

"Woke" Progressives consider the march of history to be a linear march towards a secular Utopian perfection, where the oppressive Laws of God have been repealed. It began with the New England Puritans. While Southerners were following Daniel Boone through the Cumberland Gap, these Yankee Utopians were burning witches in John Winthrop's "City upon a hill"; while Southerners were with "Old Hickory" whipping the British at New Orleans, New England Yankees were sitting at home and trading with the enemy; and while Southerners were five hundred miles west of the Mississippi in Texas defending the Alamo, these Yankee Utopians were a hundred miles west of the Hudson in New York, establishing their collectivist, Free-Love communes, and setting themselves up as the standard by which all true Americans should be measured. In this they have been remarkably successful, to the point where today they have the inmates running the asylum. But as the Preacher says in the Book of Ecclesiastes, "Consider the works of God, for who can make that straight which He hath made crooked?"

The righteous "woke" and their rent-a-thug "social justice war-riors" love to claim they are on "The Right Side of History," but Southerners know that history is not a linear march that will end in a rosy Utopian dream. It is a cyclic March of Folly where rosy Utopian dreams end in totalitarian nightmares.

I.

Blame Abraham Lincoln

*Slavery has nothing whatever to do
with the tremendous issues now awaiting
decision. It has disappeared almost
entirely from the political discussions of the day.
No one mentions it in connection with our
present complications. The question which we
have to meet is precisely what it would be if there
were not a negro slave on American soil...*

— New York Times, *quoted in the
Richmond Whig, April 9, 1861.*

GEORGE ORWELL, in his dystopian novel *1984*, wrote that "Ignorance is strength." Big Brother thrives on it—whether in a totalitarian despotism or in a universal suffrage democracy orchestrated by demagogues. In his government schools it is easy and politically profitable for Big Brother to teach ignorance—the foundation of credulous indoctrination—with simplistic *flash cards*. Take for example the "Civil War," one of the defining events in American History:

Card #1: The War was fought over slavery.

Card #2: Lincoln freed the slaves.

Card #3: End of Story—Any Questions?

1

Well, yes. Wars are not fought over other peoples' labor systems. They are fought over the control of resources. May we bring up the *flash cards* for Algebraic Equations and apply them to a comparison between England's War to Prevent the American Colonies' Independence in 1776 and the United States' War to Prevent the Southern States' Independence in 1861? Please pay attention as we develop these cards, which will be based upon an understanding of Mercantilism as an economic system for the control of resources.

A Mercantile system is an economic system comprised of an industrial and financial center, or "Core," that directs the operation of the system, and an outlying agricultural and mining "Periphery" which provides the Core with primary products for manufacturing and markets for its finished products. This system may be expressed algebraically as:

$$M = C + P$$

where M represents the mercantile system itself, and C and P represent the Core and Periphery respectively, the two major components that comprise the system.

With the coming of the Industrial Revolution, Mercantilism (M) replaced Feudalism in Europe as the primary economic system for controlling resources, classic examples being the Core European Powers (C) and their Peripheral "New World" colonies (P).

While a mercantile system may originate with mutual benefit to both of its parts, the system eventually develops a trade imbalance which is favorable to the Core at the expense of the Periphery. This is illustrated by the Argentine Economist Raul Prebisch's *Dependency Theory*. Prebisch argues that the concentration of exports in primary commodities (raw materials) from the Periphery has a structural tendency to deteriorate the terms of trade, because the price of primary commodities exported from the Periphery rises more slowly than the cost of manufactured commodities imported from the Core. Thus, the wealth of the Periphery gravitates towards the Core as profits, creating the trade imbalance against the Periphery. The Core—which then controls the system—becomes imperialistic, dictates economic policy, and exploits the Periphery as its economic "colony."[22]

That is what happened in the British mercantile system in 1776—(examples like the tax on tea, "taxation without representation," and "The Boston Tea Party" come to mind)—driving the thirteen colonies to secede from the Empire and driving Britain to wage a war against them to prevent it. After the war, New England (and eventually the industrializing Northeast as a whole, with its growing sectional majorities and its tendency to centralize the powers of the Federal Government into its own hands) developed the same mercantile relationship towards her sister agricultural States in the South that England had previously enjoyed with her colonies.[23] In both cases the balance of trade became exploitative against the Periphery. In both cases it drove the Periphery to secession (-P) from the Core-controlled economic system. In both cases it drove the Core (C) to launch a war (W) of conquest against the Periphery in an attempt to drive it back under the Core's control. These wars may each be expressed by the Algebraic Equation:

$$C - P = W$$

Where C (the Core) - P (the secession of the Periphery) = W (War). Applied specifically, we have C (England) - P (the secession of the Thirteen American Colonies) = W (the War of 1776) and C (The United States) - P (the secession of the Confederate States) = W (the War of 1861).

So, what about slavery and emancipation? Chattel slavery is as old as recorded history. It appeared with the Agricultural Revolution, when Adam was driven out of the Garden of Eden and learned the domestication of plants and animals. This was the foundation of all the ancient civilizations, all of which practiced slavery. In the middle of the nineteenth century, with the coming of the Industrial Revolution, steam power and mechanization were replacing muscle power as the prime mover of civilization, and slavery (an inefficient and therefore unprofitable labor system in industrializing societies) was ending all over the world through natural technological and economic dictates without the necessity of war. But in both of the cases we are discussing, the Periphery (the Thirteen Colonies in 1776 and the Southern States in 1861) employed slave labor P(S). In both cases, the Core (by Lord Dunmore in 1775 and Abraham Lincoln in 1863) issued a limited emancipation proclamation C(E) as a war measure directed solely and specifically against the slave-holding Periphery with whom they were at war. Factor these into each equation as a mathematical constant and we have:

$$C(E) - P(S) = W(1776), \text{ and } C(E) - P(S) = W(1861)$$

If the factors on the left of each equation are the same, then those on the right are the same. Factor out C(E) - P(S) as a constant in both equations and we have:

$$W(1776) = W(1861)$$

Like George III, Lincoln waged a war of conquest, not of liberation. With the South's "Cotton Kingdom" out from under the control of the North's "Mercantile Kingdom" and set up as a free trade confederation on her southern doorstep and in control of the mouth of the Mississippi, which drained the heartland of the United States, the economic fortunes of the North would have collapsed, so Lincoln (*a la* George III) launched his war of invasion, conquest, and coerced political allegiance against the Southern States to drive them back into the Union and under the North's control. The Confederacy was the American Empire's first conquest, and the slavery issue was merely the smelly red herring dragged across the tracks of Yankee imperialism and Puritan hubris.

II.

Virginia's Decision In 1861

*If the Union were to undertake to enforce
by arms the allegiance of the confederate States
by military means, it would be in a position
very analogous to that of England at the
time of the War of Independence.*

—*Alexis de Tocqueville, from* Democracy in America[24]

ON JANUARY 7, 1861, Virginia's Governor John Letcher con-
vened the Virginia General Assembly in extra session because of
the extraordinary situation of the secession from the Union of the
State of South Carolina at the election of Abraham Lincoln to the
Presidency—a lawyer and railroad lobbyist, and the candidate of
a strictly sectional Northern political party in vocal and vitriolic
enmity against the South. In the evening session of that same date,
delegate Wyndham Robertson, who had once served as Governor
of Virginia, presented to the House of Delegates what came to be
known as the Anti-Coercion Resolution:

> *Mr. Robertson, from the committee to whom was
> referred so much of the governor's message as re-
> lates to the coercion of a state by the general gov-
> ernment, presented the following resolutions:*
>
> "**Resolved** by the general assembly of Virginia,
> that the Union being formed by the assent of the

sovereign states respectively, and being consistent only with freedom and the republican institutions guaranteed to each, cannot and ought not to be maintained by force.

Resolved, that the government of the Union has no power to declare or make war against any of the states which have been its constituent members.

Resolved, that when any one or more of the states has determined or shall determine, under existing circumstances, to withdraw from the Union, we are unalterably opposed to any attempt on the part of the federal government to coerce the same into reunion or submission, and that we will resist the same by all the means in our power.

On motion of Mr. Seddon, the vote was recorded as follows: Ayes: 112; Noes: 5.[25]

When the secession crisis arose, Virginia, "The Mother of States and of Statesmen," called a Peace Conference of all States to try to resolve the differences between the two sections and to hold the voluntary Union of sovereign States together that she and her statesmen had done so much to create. But Virginia told the Lincoln Administration in no uncertain terms that, while she thought the secession of the seven "Cotton States" was a mistake and unnecessary, they were fully within their rights, and she would not condone any coercion of those States by his administration to force them to return to the Union, warning him that any such attempt would lead to war.

Lincoln did not listen to the counsel of Virginia. He listened instead to his constituents in the industrializing North who had gotten him elected, and whose money interests would suffer or even collapse if the agricultural South—and particularly the "Cotton Kingdom"—were allowed to leave the Union and out from under the control of their "Mercantile Kingdom." Lincoln therefore rebuffed all Southern overtures of diplomacy, and instead sent a heavily armed armada to Charleston to provoke the South into firing the first shot and get the war he and his moneyed constituents wanted. After the success of his plan, he wrote to the commander of the expedition, Capt. G.V. Fox:

> You and I both anticipated that the cause of the country would be advanced by making the attempt to provision Ft. Sumter, *even if it should fail*; and it is no small consolation now to feel that *our anticipation is justified by the result.*(26)[26]

Lincoln then called for a quota of troops from each of the respective States—without the consent of Congress (which, under Article I, sect. 8 of the Constitution, has the sole power to declare war)—to drive the "Cotton States" back into the Union at the point of the bayonet. Lincoln, the obfuscating lawyer, got around the Constitution by declaring that he was merely calling for troops to put down "a rebellion too large to be contained by U.S. Marshalls"—perhaps the greatest understatement in the history of the world. And since Lincoln did not recognize that the seceded States were out of the Union, by this masterful splitting of a hair he also absolved himself of treason (under Article III, sect. 3) for invading the Southern States with his armies. But "The Mother of States and of Statesmen" did not absolve him, for she was not taken in by his specious legalisms. She knew what despotism looked like, for she had seen the same thing from King George III "four-score and seven years" earlier. When Virginia received Lincoln's demand for troops, Governor Letcher was astonished, and he emphatically refused to comply. A copy of his response may be found in the Richmond *Enquirer*, April 18, 1861:

Executive Department

Richmond, Va. April 16th, 1861

Hon. Simon Cameron, Secretary of War.

Sir: I received your telegram of the 15th, the genuineness of which I doubted. Since that time, I have received your communication, mailed the same day, in which I am requested to detach from the militia of the State of Virginia 'the quota designated in a table,' which you append, 'to serve as infantry or riflemen for the period of three months, unless sooner discharged.'

In reply to this communication, I have only to say, that the militia of Virginia will not be furnished to the powers at Washington, for any such use or purpose as they have in view. Your object is to subjugate the Southern States, and a requisition made upon me for such an object—an object, in my judgment, not within the purview of the Constitution, or the act of 1795—will not be complied with. You have chosen to inaugurate civil war, and having done so, we will meet it, in a spirit as determined as the Administration has exhibited towards the South.

Respectfully, John Letcher

The next day, April 17, 1861, the Virginia Convention, which had recently voted overwhelmingly to remain in the Union, passed Virginia's *Ordinance of Secession*. Virginia subsequently joined the Southern Confederacy. Four other States (including occupied Missouri) followed her out. As Winston Churchill wrote:

Upon Lincoln's call to arms to coerce the seceding states Virginia made without hesitation the choice which she was so heroically to sustain. She would not fight on the issue of slavery, but stood firm on the constitutional ground that every state in the Union enjoyed sovereign rights. On this principle Virginians denied the claim of the Federal Government to exercise coercion. By eighty-eight votes to fifty-five the Virginia Convention at Richmond refused to allow the state militia to respond to Lincoln's call. Virginia seceded from the Union and placed her entire military forces at the disposal of the Confederacy. This decided the conduct of [Robert E. Lee,] one of the noblest Americans who ever lived, and one of the greatest captains known to the annals of war...[27]

And as Thomas Carlyle said, "It takes men of worth to recognize worth in men."[28]

III.

Is Secession Treason?

Hamlet. *Is not Parchment made of sheep-skins?*

Horatio. *Ay, my lord, and of calf-skins, too.*

Hamlet. *They are sheep and calves which seek out assurance in that...*

—Hamlet, Act V, Sc. 1

THE U.S. SUPREME COURT, in *Texas v. White* (1869), ruled that a sovereign State's secession from the voluntary Union of States was unconstitutional. Chief Justice Salmon P. Chase wrote the "opinion of the court" (which was not unanimous). His opinion blatantly discounted the *Declaration of Independence*, which states:

> "Governments long established should not be changed for light and transient causes... But when a long train of abuses and usurpations, pursuing invariably the same Object, evinces a design to reduce them under absolute Despotism, it is their right, it is their duty, to throw off such Government, and to provide new Guards for their future security..."[29]

Chase's opinion also blatantly discounted the plainly stated condition upon which Virginia joined the Union when the Virginia Convention ratified the Constitution:

> "We the Delegates of the People of Virginia ... Do in the name and in behalf of the People of Virginia declare and make known that the powers granted under the Constitution being derived from the People of the United States may be resumed by them whensoever the same shall be perverted to their injury or oppression..."[30]

Chase's opinion further blatantly ignored the stated condition upon which New York joined the Union when the New York Convention ratified the Constitution:

> "We the Delegates of the People of the State of New York ... Do declare and make known ... That all Power is originally vested in and consequently derived from the People, and that Government is instituted by them for their common Interest, Protection, and Security... That the Powers of Government may be reassumed by the People, whensoever it shall become necessary..."[31]

Chase also dismissed the opinion of the New England States in their Hartford Convention in 1814, when they threatened secession over the War of 1812, dismissed the opinion of the Northern States that, at one time or another, threatened secession over the Fugitive Slave Law, the Mexican War, and the admission of Texas, and dismissed the opinion of the Radical Abolitionists who loudly clamored for "No Union with slaveholders!"[32] Furthermore, it went without saying that his opinion was certainly not that of the States of the Southern Confederacy that did in fact secede. Nor was it the opinion of the many Northern newspaper editors who were thrown into prison without trial for expressing this opinion, and who had their presses destroyed by the army when Lincoln unconstitutionally suspended the writ of *habeas corpus* while waging his unconstitutional war, all in violation of Article I, section 8 and 9; Article III, section 3; and the First and Tenth Amendments to the Constitution (although all have since been cleverly obfuscated by the Lincoln sycophants, cultists, and "Court Historians").[33]

While there were those of the Hamilton-Clay-Webster persuasion who wanted a stronger centralized government, the Jeffersonian States' Rights view of the Constitution prevailed until 1865. Before the war, the Constitution limited the powers of the General Government and guaranteed the reserved powers to the States, but Lincoln's War and the Reconstruction that followed was a Radical Revolution, a bloody and murderous usurpation of power that transformed the voluntary Union of sovereign States created by the States themselves, into a coerced Empire pinned together by bayonets that relegated the once-sovereign States into provinces under its imperial dominion.

Before the war, the General Government was made to conform to the Constitution. After the war, the Constitution was made to conform to the General Government, and *Texas v. White* (1869) was just one of the many rotten fruits that fell from the corrupt tree of Radical Reconstruction. Thomas Jefferson warned of it at least as far back as 1820 in a letter to William Charles Jarvis:

> "You seem ... to consider the judges as the ultimate arbiters of all constitutional questions; a very dangerous doctrine indeed, and one which would place us under the despotism of an oligarchy. Our judges are as honest as other men, and not more so. They have, with others, the same passions for party, for power, and the privilege of their corps. Their maxim is *"boni judicis est ampliare jurisdictionem"* [good justice is broad jurisdiction], and their power the more dangerous as they are in office for life, and not responsible, as the other functionaries are, to the elective control. The Constitution has erected no such single tribunal, knowing that to whatever

hands confided, with the corruptions of time and party, its members would become despots..."[34]

This warning became prophesy during the Radical Reconstruction after the war, when Chief Justice Salmon P. Chase followed Lincoln's lead in the exercise of arbitrary power.

Who was Chief Justice Salmon P. Chase and how did he come to the opinion that secession is unconstitutional in *Texas v. White* in 1869? Chase was well-known as a Radical Republican[35] who had been Lincoln's Secretary of the Treasury and who had called for military action against Ft. Sumter.[36] He evidently was a man of expediency when it came to money. In 1862, he endorsed Lincoln's government—created fiat money known as "greenbacks" to finance the war rather than have the government borrow money from the big money bankers. The Money Trust on Wall Street, of course, didn't like greenbacks because they couldn't control the money supply or make any money off of them, so Wall Street sent Secretary of the Treasury Chase to Congress to "recommend" the creation of the Second National Bank of 1863, which would undercut the greenbacks and sell the monetary independence of the United States Government to the Money Trust, letting them, rather than the government, create the money (and then loan it at interest to the government.) Chase engineered the sellout, and Lincoln got rid of him by making him Chief Justice of the Supreme Court in 1864.[37]

Salmon P. Chase was a blessing to Wall Street as Secretary of the Treasury. Now, as Chief Justice of the Supreme Court, what other favors could he bestow? He could rule secession unconstitutional for them. Wall Street had calculated previously the profits of secession, knowing that it would bring on war (and wealth to Wall Street from government-issued bonds to finance it with), so they had stoked the flames of hatred by helping to finance Harriet Beecher Stowe's *Uncle Tom's Cabin*, the *Dred Scott* case, the issue of slavery in the Territories, "Bleeding Kansas," John Brown's Raid on Harper's Ferry, and the media and the politicians who fanned those flames of hatred, which had finally brought on the secession of the Cotton States. But cotton was "King" at the time, and if the

South's "Cotton Kingdom" were out of the Union and free trading with Europe, the North's "Mercantile Kingdom" would collapse. Wall Street knew that Lincoln would wage war to prevent this.[38] The gamble was that if the Confederate States won their independence, they could repudiate their debts, and the banks would not be able to foreclose on them. But with the overwhelming industrial might of the North, a Naval blockade to starve out the South and keep Europe from interfering, and endless hordes of immigrants from European ghettoes pouring into New York and Philadelphia to be recruited with liberal bounties to fill up the ranks of the Union Armies with mercenaries, the Confederacy wouldn't stand a chance, so Lincoln launched his armada against Charleston to provoke the South into firing the first shot and got the war he wanted.[39] After four years of the bloodiest war in the history of the Western Hemisphere, Lincoln drove the "Cotton Kingdom" back into the Union, but it had been a close thing. Now, with Radical Reconstruction cementing the Southern States back under the control of the North,[40] there only lacked a ruling by the Supreme Court to make secession unconstitutional to put the shackles on the Southern States for good, and Chief Justice Salmon P. Chase was their man.

Confederate President Jefferson Davis (who was vindictively imprisoned in chains at Ft. Monroe for two years) was to be tried for treason by military tribunal and hanged, but the civil courts had been restored and prosecutors started dragging their feet. They feared that charges of treason against Davis would expose them to the fact that the Constitution nowhere prohibited the peaceful withdrawal of a State from the voluntary Union that the States themselves had founded. It might also bring up the fact that Abraham Lincoln, who had not recognized the Confederate States as being out of the Union, had committed treason under Article III, section 3 of the Constitution when he invaded them. If this were to happen, it would expose Lincoln's War as the war of conquest that it was, rather than a war ostensibly to "suppress rebellion." The government would lose in court what it had won on the battlefield, so Chief Justice Chase quietly had the case dropped on a technicality and President Davis was released on bond, "un-reconstructed" to the end.[41]

While the chance was missed in the case of Jefferson Davis, Chase had another opportunity in the case of *Texas v. White* in 1869. It involved ten million dollars of bonds given to Texas during the Compromise of 1850. Radical Reconstruction was still in full swing, with the Southern States *in* the Union for the sake of plunder, but *out* of the Union for any Constitutional redress. The North's astronomical national debt service had to be paid, and the Wall Street Money Trust stood to lose money in the future if Texas secession (and thereby that of any other State) was ruled to be Constitutional, just as the North's "Mercantile Kingdom" would have suffered financial disaster if the South's "Cotton Kingdom" had been allowed out of the Union. The Chief Justice, using specious arguments of Daniel Webster, ruled that since the old Articles of Confederation made the Union under the Confederation "perpetual," and since the Preamble of the new Constitution made the Union "more perfect," therefore the Union was an "indestructible Union of Indestructible States," which made secession unconstitutional.[42]

The Union under the old Articles of Confederation was indeed deemed "perpetual," yet the States in that Union seceded from it under Art. VII of the Constitution of the new and "more perfect" Union. As John Remington Graham—former law professor, experienced trial lawyer, and specialist in British, American, and Canadian constitutional law and history—wrote in his work *Blood Money*: "The Union is perpetual, as a corporation can be perpetual, which means only that it is not limited by a term of years, and so will last forever unless lawfully dissolved." He goes on to say that under the "more perfect" Union created by the new Constitution, "No longer may secession be effected by legislative act of a State as under the Articles of Confederation. Under the intended meaning of the United States Constitution, only the people of a State in convention may effect withdrawal from the Union, which, consequently, is more perfect."[43] Thomas Jefferson, the author of *The Kentucky Resolutions*, would have agreed:

"[T]he several States composing the United States of America, are not united on the principles of unlimited submission to their General Government; but that by compact under the style and title of a Constitution for the United States and of amendments thereto, they constituted a General Government for special purposes, delegated to that Government certain definite powers, reserving each State to itself the residuary mass of right to their own self Government... [T]he Government created by this compact was not made the exclusive or final *judge* of the extent of the powers delegated to itself; since that would have made its discretion, and not the Constitution, the measure of its powers..."[44]

Having just won their independence from Britain; the citizens of the new Republic could hardly have been expected to entrust their hard-won liberties to a half-dozen lawyers who had been appointed judges-for-life by some politician. But that all changed with Lincoln's revolution. With the Supreme Court (rather than the States which created the Federal Government and its Charter) now as the final arbiter of all Constitutional questions, including those limiting the powers of the Federal Government, and with the Supreme Court being part of the Federal Government, the Federal Government, therefore, is now the final arbiter of the limits of its own power—and that, said Jefferson, is the very definition of despotism! Instead of offering his obfuscating legalese and pettifoggery for the unconstitutionality of secession in *Texas v. White*, Chief Justice Salmon P. Chase could have simply said "Secession is treason because we won the war."

IV.

The "Myth" of the Lost Cause

History is the propaganda of the victorious.
—Voltaire

AN AFRICAN-AMERICAN COLUMNIST at the Richmond *Times-Dispatch* (who was awarded the Pulitzer Prize for "helping us get through the Confederate Monument crisis in Richmond" or something) recently opined that it is time to "unlearn" the "fake history" of The Lost Cause and slavery that he claims has been taught in schools across Virginia and the South. Let us address these two points separately, remembering that the "History Book" is one of the spoils of war.

The South is the Apostate in John Winthrop's shining "City upon a Hill," and the Southern Confederacy is the scapegoat for all its sins. The political "hue and cry" against all things Confederate by our Latter-day Puritans is based upon their specious charge that they commemorate the "Lost Cause" of treason, slavery, and racism—which is a classic example of what respected historians call "presentism": the twisting of history to conform to the politics of the day.

To accuse the Southern States of *treason* for attempting to peacefully withdraw from the voluntary Union of sovereign States that all acceded to at the Founding, or subsequently, one must first wipe one's feet on the Declaration of Independence, signed by the thirteen (slave-holding) Colonies that seceded from the British Empire in 1776. The Patriots, too, of 1776 were accused of treason, so the Confederacy stood in good company. Lincoln's invasion of the Southern States, which he did not recognize as being out of the Union, was, by his own definition, treason according to Article III, section 3 of the U.S. Constitution. Self-defense against invasion, conquest, and coerced political allegiance is not. No Confederate was ever tried for treason after the war.

To claim that the Confederacy "took up arms to destroy the Union in defense of *slavery,*" please note that no one had taken up arms against the South to end slavery. To claim otherwise, one must ignore Lincoln's emphatic disclaimer to the contrary in his First Inaugural Address,[45] and then ignore his famous *Emancipation Proclamation*, issued two years later, stating plainly that slavery was alright as long as one were loyal to his government[46]— proven by the fact that slavery was Constitutional in the United States throughout the war.

As for *racism*, please note that while slave-holding societies had "Black Codes," the first "Jim Crow" laws originated in the free Northern States, some prohibiting Blacks—either slave or free— from residing there.[47] These Northern "Jim Crow" laws showed that the North's strong objections to slavery in the Territories was based not on their moral objections to slavery, but on their objections to having Blacks in the Territories.[48] The sainted Lincoln—himself a documented White Supremacist[49]—worked until the day he died to have free Blacks deported or repatriated to Latin America or back to Africa.[50]

As for *Black racism* and *Black slavery*, remember that it was Black Africans who captured and sold Black Africans into slavery in the first place.[51] Furthermore, United States Census records in the early nineteenth century listed many free Black owners of slaves—from New Orleans to New England—some owning extensive plantations and numerous slaves.[52]

Much of today's "fake history" of slavery comes from calculated omissions in order that one might confirm one's credentials as a victim, for there is evidently a great deal of political advantage these days in "going for the gold" in the "Victimhood Olympics." Therefore, while we are "unlearning the fake history of slavery" it may be of interest to unlearn some of the "fake history" of the *victims* of slavery.

As most of our African-American citizens today are descendants of slaves imported into the United States (and would—for good or ill—still be living in Africa today had it not been for the African slave-trade) we might find of interest a portrait of the much-celebrated "Mother Africa" in the testimony of the last known individual to have been smuggled here in a slave ship just prior to the War Between the States. The noted African-American anthropologist Zora Neale Hurston recorded the testimony of Cudjo "Kossola" Lewis near Mobile, Alabama, in her book *Dust Tracks on a Road*.[53]

Lewis had been a member of the Takkoi nation. One morning his village was attacked by the fearsome Amazon warriors of Dahomey, who burst through the gates of the compound while the male warriors waited outside to seize those who fled. The old and infirm were beheaded and their heads carried off as trophies. The rest were marched in a slave coffle to the Kingdom of Dahomey and the barracoons on the beach at Dmydah. On the second day of the march the severed heads began to rot, so the African slavers halted to smoke and dry them. Lewis reported that they had to watch the drying heads of their friends and relatives turning on the long poles in the smoke.

At Dahomey, they saw the King's palace surrounded by a wall of skulls before they were put into a barracoon on the beach to await the arrival of a slave ship. There were many captive tribes there, each tribe placed in a separate barracoon to prevent them from warring with each other. When a trader arrived, he would first decide which tribe interested him, and then—with the men lined up on one side and the women on the other—he would go along picking out the slaves he wished to purchase. Lewis was embarked in the *Chlotilde*, a fast-sailing vessel built and owned by the Maher brothers of Maine, who had moved to Alabama. The vessel was chased by a British Man-o'-War on slave patrol, but she outran it. Arriving at Mobile, the vessel and cargo were smuggled into the river, the hundred-odd slaves unloaded, and the vessel scuttled. The Africans then began their brief careers as slaves in

America—some of whom may have ended up serving in some Reconstruction legislature a few years later. Such things happened in those days.

The implications of "fake history" today are that the South has a monopoly on sin, but one might note that the slave smugglers who brought Lewis and his people here were from Maine, one of the New England centers of the African slave-trade. Dr. W.E.B. DuBois, in his work *The Suppression of the African Slave Trade to the United States*, quotes the January 1862 issue of the *Continental Monthly* (available online at www.gutenberg.org; Title: The Continental Monthly, Vol. 1, No. 1, January 1862; Article: "The Slave-Trade in New York") as stating that New York, Boston, and Portland were the largest African Slave-trading ports in the world at the time.

Moreover, in her work quoted above, Zora Neale Hurston said that in spite of the fact that White people had purchased and exploited her people, the "inescapable fact that stuck in my craw, was my people had *sold* me, and the White people had bought me." She said it did away with the folklore ("fake history?") she had been brought up on, that white people had gone to Africa, waved a red handkerchief at the Africans to lure them onto the beach and aboard of the slave ship out of curiosity, and then sailed away with them. But no, she said, her own people had "butchered and killed, exterminated whole nations and torn families apart, for a profit" before strangers arrived, and all that Lewis had told her was verified from other historical sources.

While White Americans (North and South) *owned* slaves and *traded* in slaves, they did not *enslave* anyone. It was Black Africans who did that. How shall we fit that into our Pulitzer Prize winner's endeavor to "unlearn fake history"?

V.

Free Negro Owners of Slaves

From the U.S. Census of 1830, compiled by Dr. Carter G. Woodson, PhD.[54]

On the way home we passed a large plantation which, I was told, belonged to a free negro, one of the richest men of the county, who was himself the owner of numerous slaves...

—Maj. Heros von Borcke, CSA, Adjutant on Lt. Gen. J.E.B. Stuart's staff.[55]

DR. CARTER G. WOODSON (1875-1950), known as "The Father of Black History," was born in Buckingham County, Virginia, the son of former slaves. He received his doctorate from Harvard, rose in prominence as a writer and historian, and was the editor of *The Journal of Negro History*. He is best known for establishing Black History Week, which evolved into Black History Month.

In 1924, Dr. Woodson compiled from the U.S. Census records of 1830 the names and numbers of free Black owners of slaves listed by State, along with the number of slaves owned by each. The statistics were copied by three assistants under his supervision, and published in *Free Negro Owners of Slaves in the United States in 1830, Together with Absentee Ownership of Slaves in the United States in 1830* (Washington, DC: The Association for the Study of Negro Life and History, 1924).

Most of the listings are in the South, but there are also listings of free Black owners of slaves in Connecticut, Delaware, the District of Columbia, Illinois, Maine, New Hampshire, New Jersey, New York, Ohio, Pennsylvania, and Rhode Island. In the North, outside of Washington, DC, (which had 70), Pennsylvania had the most number of free Black owners of slaves, numbering twelve, with New York and New Jersey next.

In the South, the majority of free Black owners of slaves were to be found in the older States of Maryland, Virginia, South Carolina, and Louisiana. In many of these cases, Dr. Woodson says, the ownership was philanthropic, with the free husband purchasing his wife, or the free wife purchasing her husband. In many other cases the land and slave holdings of these free Blacks rivaled those of the White planters. In South Carolina, for example, there were four hundred and sixty-four free Black owners of slaves listed, ninety-nine of whom were listed as owning ten or more slaves, one of whom owned eighty-four. In Virginia, there are listed nine hundred and forty-nine free Black owners of slaves in 1830, with sixteen owning ten or more slaves, one of whom owned seventy-one. Sixty-eight free Black owners of slaves were residents of the City of Richmond proper. In all, over 2,200 slaves in Virginia in 1830 were owned by free Blacks, including over 130 in the City of Richmond.

Somehow this important research on slavery by Dr. Carter G. Woodson, "The Father of Black History," has been cast down the Orwellian "memory hole." By whom? And why?

VI.

The Myth of The Righteous Cause

Yankees Take Up the White Man's Burden

Take up the White Man's burden –

Ye dare not stoop to less –

Nor call too loud on Freedom

To cloak your weariness;

By all ye cry or whisper,

By all ye leave or do,

The silent, sullen peoples

Shall weigh your Gods and you...

—Rudyard Kipling, from *The White Man's Burden*[56]

AFRICAN SLAVES WERE FIRST brought to the New World in 1503 to the Island of Hispaniola. Eventually all of the commercial European nations were involved in the trade, and all of their colonies in the Americas were supplied with them. Virginia received her first shipment from a Dutch Man o' War in 1619, (which shipment Virginia purchased as indentured servants—the same as with European indentured servants), but the share of Virginia in the African slave trade was that of an unwilling recipient, not an active participant. Virginia's obedience to the subsequent laws of her governors and citizens, and of the Colonial laws of England prevented her from trading to foreign ports. The carrying trade was left to Englishmen and to the illicit trade of the commercial Colonies of New England.[57]

The pious "Puritan Fathers" of Massachusetts got into slavery early on with the enslavement of the Indians, but quickly got into the African slave-trade within twenty years after landing at Plymouth Rock. As The Reverend Robert Louis Dabney noted, "[I]t may be correctly said, that the commerce of New England was born of the slave trade; as its subsequent prosperity was largely founded upon it... The towns of Providence, Newport, and New Haven became famous slave trading ports. The magnificent harbor of the second, especially, was the favorite starting-place of the slave ships... When it is remembered that the Massachusetts ports were then small towns, the fact that they had more than twenty ships simultaneously engaged in the trade to the Guinea coast alone, clearly reveals that it was the leading branch of their maritime adventure, and main source of their wealth."[58] Even after the trade was outlawed in the Constitution in 1809, New York, Boston, and Portland were the largest African slave trading ports in the world—doing illicit trading with Cuba and Brazil—when Lincoln took his oath of office.[59]

Virginia, on the other hand, from its inception always denounced and endeavored to restrict the trade, but without success due to the vetoes of the English Crown. However, after the War for Independence, Virginia was the first country in the history of the world to abolish the African slave-trade.[60] As Dr. Dabney noted, "It is one of the strange freaks of history that this commonwealth, which was guiltless in this thing, and which always presented a steady protest against the enormity, should become, in spite of herself, the home of the largest number of African slaves found within any of the States, and thus, should be held up by Abolitionists as the representative of the 'sin of slaveholding;' while Massachusetts, which was, next to England, the pioneer and patroness of the slave trade, and chief criminal, having gained for her share the wages of iniquity instead of the persons of the victims, has arrogated to herself the post of chief accuser of Virginia..."[61]

But as John Randolph of Roanoke said, blood will tell in a four-mile heat.[62] The "four-mile heat" was run in 1861–1865, and both the blood of the Puritan and his altruism for the Black people showed itself in full relief...

Edward A. Pollard, editor of the Richmond *Examiner* during the war, reported, "The fact is indisputable, that in all the localities of the Confederacy where the enemy had obtained a foothold, the negroes had been reduced by mortality during the war to not more than one-half their previous number... In the winter of 1863–64, the Governor of Louisiana, in his official message, published to the world the appalling fact, that *more negroes had perished in Louisiana from the cruelty and brutality of the public enemy than the combined number of white men, in both armies, from the casualties of war.* In illustration, he stated that when the Confederate forces surprised and captured Berwick's Bay, last summer, they found about two thousand negroes there in a state of the most utter destitution—many of them so emaciated and sick that they died before the tender humanity of the Confederates could be applied to their rescue from death. The fate of these poor wretches was to be attributed to sheer inhumanity. The Yankees had abundant supplies of food, medicines, and clothing at hand, but they did not apply them to the comfort of the negro, who, once entitled to the farce of "freedom," was of no more consequence to them than any other beast with a certain amount of useful labor in his anatomy."[63]

William Faulkner paints a portrait of it in *The Unvanquished*, of the burning houses, barns and gins, and the countless numbers of Blacks passing along the roads day and night following the Yankee armies to the Promised Land, singing and raising clouds of dust that didn't settle for days: "[W]e sat up listening to them, and the next morning every few yards along the road would be the old ones who couldn't keep up anymore, sitting or lying down and even crawling along, calling to the others to help them, and the others, the young ones, not stopping, not even looking at them; I don't think they even heard or saw them. Going to Jordan, they told me. Going to cross Jordan..."—and stopped at the river by the Yankee cavalry, who were to blow the bridge to keep them from crossing and following the army.[64] Faulkner's portrait of Sherman in Mississippi had a documented counterpart in Sherman's march through Georgia, when his Engineers were ordered to cut loose the pontoon bridge over the unfordable Ebenezer Creek to keep the horde of Blacks from following his army. Many Blacks stampeded and drowned in the icy waters trying to swim across.[65]

Edward A. Pollard continues: "The practice of the enemy in the parts of the Confederacy he had invaded, was to separate the families of the blacks without notice. Governor Moore officially testified to this practice in Louisiana. The men were driven off like so many cattle to a Yankee camp, and were enlisted in the Yankee army. The women and children were likewise driven off in droves, and put upon what are called 'Government plantations'—that is, plantations from which the lawful owners had been forced to fly, and which the Yankees in Louisiana were cultivating. The condition of the negroes at the various contraband camps in the Mississippi valley furnishes a terrible volume of human misery, which may someday be written in the frightful characters of truth. Congregated at these depots, without employment, deprived of the food to which they had been accustomed, and often without shelter or medical care, these helpless creatures perished, swept off by pestilence or the cruelties of the Yankees.[66]

"We may take from *Northern* sources some accounts of these contraband camps, to give the reader a passing picture of what the unhappy negroes had gained by what the Yankees called their 'freedom.' A letter to a Massachusetts paper said: 'There are, between Memphis and Natchez, not less than fifty thousand blacks, from among whom have been culled all able-bodied men for the military service. Thirty-five thousand of these, viz., those in camps between Helena and Natchez, are furnished the shelter of old tents and subsistence of cheap rations by the Government, but are in all other things in extreme destitution. Their clothing, in perhaps the case of a fourth of this number, is but one single worn and scanty garment. Many children are wrapped night and day in tattered blankets as their sole apparel. But few of all these people have had any change of raiment since, in midsummer or earlier, they came from the abandoned plantations of their masters. Multitudes of them have no beds or bedding—the clayey earth the resting place of women and babes through these stormy winter months. They live of necessity in extreme filthiness, and are afflicted with all fatal diseases. Medical attendance and supplies are very inadequate. They cannot, during the winter, be disposed to labor and self-support, and compensated labor cannot be procured for them in the camps. They cannot, in their present condition, survive the winter. It is my conviction that, unrelieved, the half of them will perish before the spring. Last winter, during the months of February, March, and April, I buried, at Memphis alone, out of an average of about four thousand, twelve hundred of these people, or twelve a day..."'[67]

Pollard goes on to write: "In all the war there had been no servile insurrection in the South—not a single instance of outbreak among the slaves—a conclusive evidence that the negro was not the enemy of his master, but, in his desertion of him, merely the victim of Yankee bribes. Assured, through a thousand channels, as these negroes were, that they were the victims of the most grinding and cruel injustice and oppression; assured of the active assistance of the largest armies of modern times, and of the countenance and sympathy of the rest of the world; assured that such an enterprise would not only be generous and heroic, but eminently successful, our enemies had heretofore failed to excite one solitary instance of insurrection, much less to bring on a servile war. It was thus that the war itself had greatly cleared up our moral atmosphere, and swept away much mist and darkness of doubt and delusion. After nearly three years of bloody struggle, we had at least already attained this result: the assurance that it was we, the Confederates, who had in charge the cause of freedom in the Western continent against the wild anarchy of ignorant mobs—we, who were saving civilization from the frenzy of democracy run mad—we, above all, who were guarding the helpless black race from utter annihilation at the hands of a greedy and bloody 'philanthropy,' which sought to deprive them of the care of human masters only that they might be abolished from the face of the earth, and leave the fields of labor clear for that free competition and demand-and-supply, which reduced even white workers to the lowest *minimum* of a miserable livelihood..."[68]

While many Northerners' main concern for the newly emancipated Blacks was that they not come North to compete with them for their jobs or mingle in their society, the Radical Abolitionists in Washington had quite another view of the matter, which, far from any altruism, stemmed from their political calculations for gaining power for themselves. It has evidently taken a hundred and sixty years for some people to realize that Abraham Lincoln's war was waged not for the slave but against his master, who had been the States' Rights stumbling block thwarting Northern political ambitions for an unconstitutionally powerful central government under Northern control ever since the days of Thomas Jefferson.

With the election of Abraham Lincoln and his strictly sectional Northern political party in vitriolic enmity against the South, their political ambitions were on the verge of being realized—but their financial ambitions were suddenly met with the threat of disaster when the Southern States withdrew from the Union! Cotton was "King" in those days, and the industrializing North depended on it for her textile mills. With the "Cotton Kingdom" out of the Union and free trading with Europe, the North's "Mercantile Kingdom" would collapse into economic ruin and social anarchy, so Lincoln launched his war to drive the "Cotton Kingdom" back into the Union at the point of the bayonet. But how were the Radicals of his party to save the cotton and at the same time get rid of the Southern Planter and his politics that were the stumbling block to their political ambitions for power? According to the rare book by Otto Eisenschiml, entitled *Why Was Lincoln Murdered*,[69] the plan was as follows:

1) Let the war go on until necessity made the emancipation of the Southern slaves a war issue. This would ruin the Southern planter and remove him from the political equation, but plenty of cotton could still be had from impoverished sharecroppers—both Black and White—in the modern form of slavery known as debt peonage (which was slavery to capital, where "Ole Marster" would merely be replaced by a Northern banker.[70]

2) After the war was won, place the South under military occupation and pass Reconstruction Acts that would disfranchise the Southern Whites and enfranchise the Southern (but not Northern) Blacks.

3) Then use the Union Leagues to teach these newly enfranchised Blacks to hate "Ole Marster" and to vote for the carpetbaggers, giving the Northern political party the electoral votes of the Southern States and the political power they coveted.

The plan was sweeping in its execution, but simple in its concept, and in the end it worked perfectly. The only threat to their plan was Lincoln's proposed leniency towards the defeated South, but John Wilkes Booth took care of that problem for them.

VII.

Tools of Power

African-Americans and the
Radical Reconstruction of Virginia 1865–1870

*Was ever feather so lightly blown to
and fro as this multitude?*

—*Henry VI, Part Two, Act IV. Sc. 8.*

FOR FOUR YEARS LINCOLN'S ARMIES marched in total war across the South to the tune of the militantly Puritanical "Battle Hymn of the Republic"—burning, pillaging, raping, and killing—and drove the Southern States back into the Union at the point of the bayonet. His lofty rhetoric in his *Gettysburg Address*—claiming his war of invasion, conquest, and coerced political allegiance was in order to save "government of the people by the people for the people"[71]—is pure Orwellian doublespeak, while his *Emancipation Proclamation*—a desperate war measure issued halfway through the war when the South was winning it—plainly stated that slavery was all right as long as one was loyal to his government.[72] But that exposes *The Myth of the Righteous Cause* as a "red herring" masking a murderous usurpation of Power. As a result, any attempt by the South to expose the truth—that the slavery issue was just one among many stated reasons for secession, but that *secession itself* was what Lincoln's War was "about," when Lincoln refused to let the Southern States go in peace—is derided and dismissed as "*The*

Myth of the Lost Cause." It has so corrupted our culture that even the Virginia Historical Society's web site obfuscates the obvious truth when it states that the "Lost Cause" narrative was "developed by former Confederates who claimed that states' rights, not slavery, caused the war; that enslaved blacks remained faithful to their masters; and that the South was defeated only by overwhelming numerical and industrial strength..."[73]

Paul Kennedy, in his book *The Rise and Fall of the Great Powers*, debunks the Virginia Historical Society's scalawag narrative by detailing the North's "overwhelming numbers and resources," making the truth of the "Lost Cause" narrative abundantly clear: a Northern White population over three times that of the South steadily augmented by immigration; a Union army over twice the size of the Confederate; over six times more manufacturing establishments in the North, with fifteen times more tonnage of pig iron produced; a massive expansion of home manufactured rifles in the North against an ever-dwindling supply of rifles imported from Europe by Southern "blockade runners" through an ever-tightening Union Naval blockade; two-and-a-half times more railroad track mileage steadily expanding in the North while Southern railways were being destroyed; and 671 Union warships—including 236 steam vessels built during the war—gaining control of Southern rivers and blockading the Southern coast, while the Confederacy had virtually no Navy other than blockade runners, a few commerce raiders on the high seas, and a few ironclads bottled up in port.[74] This was underscored in Abraham Lincoln's December 1864 Message to Congress, in which he stated that "we have more men now than we had when the war began; that we are not exhausted, nor in the process of exhaustion; that we are gaining strength, and may, if need be, maintain the contest indefinitely."[75] This, with Hood's Army of Tennessee—outnumbered two-to-one by the Army of the Cumberland wrecked before Nashville; with Atlanta burned; with Sherman's 90,000 marching through Georgia to the sea in a sixty-mile-wide swath of destruction virtually unopposed before turning to his vindictive destruction of South Carolina and his projected march northward to join Grant's colossal army investing Richmond and Petersburg; and with General Lee's ragged, starving, and barefooted remnant of the Army of Northern Virginia holding thirty-two miles of frozen entrenchments from the Chickahominy to Hatcher's Run. When Lee's lines were finally broken in the Spring of 1865, his army retreated westward until it was brought to bay at Appomattox Court House. After the Surrender, Lee issued his "Farewell Address" to his men: "After four years of arduous service, marked by unsurpassed courage and fortitude, the Army of Northern Virginia has been compelled to yield to overwhelming numbers and resources..."[76] and General Lee never put a political spin on anything.

Lt. E.M. Boykin, 7th South Carolina Cavalry, gave the tally: "We stacked eight thousand stand of arms, all told; artillery, cavalry, infantry stragglers, wagon rats, and all the rest, from twelve to fifteen thousand men. The United States troops, by their own estimate, were 150,000 men, with a railroad connecting their rear with Washington, New York, Germany, France, Belgium, Africa, 'all the world and the rest of mankind,' as General Taylor comprehensively remarked, for their recruiting stations were all over the world, and the crusade against the south, and its peculiar manners and civilization, under the pressure of the 'almighty American dollar,' was as absolute and varied in its nationality as was that of 'Peter the Hermit,' under the pressure of religious zeal, upon Jerusalem..."[77] But Winston Churchill, in his monumental four-volume work entitled *A History of the English Speaking Peoples*, sums it all up with a clear and unbiased picture of not only the disparity between the combatants, but of the loyalty of the slaves until the Yankee armies marched through: "Twenty-three states, with a population of twenty-two millions, were arrayed against eleven states, whose population of nine millions included nearly four million slaves... Most of the slaves, who might have been expected to prove an embarrassment to the South, on the contrary proved a solid help, tending the plantations in the absence of their masters, raising the crops which fed the armies, working on the roads and building fortifications, thus releasing a large number of whites for service in the field"[78].

The loyalty of the slaves during the war made for treasured stories in Southern family lore and headaches for the Lincoln war effort, while after the war it caused political problems for the carpetbaggers and the Radical Republicans during Reconstruction. They needed the votes of the newly freed Blacks to cement their political control over the conquered Southern States. It took them two years to accomplish this, using the time-honored political tactic of "divide and rule"—in this case by manufacturing liberal doses of racial hatred, as we shall see.

During the war, Lincoln had recognized the Virginia Unionist government of Governor Francis H. Pierpont, which consisted of Pierpont as so-called "governor," and thirteen or so others acting as the so-called "General Assembly of Virginia." Their domain encompassed the Cities of Alexandria and Fairfax, a stone's throw across the Potomac from Washington, but this farce gave Lincoln "Constitutional permission" to divide "West Virginia" from Virginia in 1863, giving him West Virginia's electoral votes in 1864. After Lincoln's assassination, President Johnson decided to use the Pierpont government, naming Pierpont as the provisional Governor of Virginia, and subjecting him to the Federal military authorities of the State. Pierpont called for an October election for both the Virginia General Assembly and for Virginia's representatives in the U.S. Congress.[79]

In December 1865, the Virginia General Assembly and the U.S. Congress met on the same day, but the Virginia and other Southern State representatives to the U.S. Congress could not take the oath prescribed by the Radicals, and they were not allowed to take their seats.[80] The Northern Radicals were in control, and they intended to keep it that way. Representative Thaddeus Stevens stated: "The future condition of the conquered power depends on the will of the conqueror. They must come in as new States or remain as conquered provinces. Congress ... is the only power that can act in the matter... Congress must create States and declare when they are entitled to be represented... As there are no symptoms that the people of these provinces will be prepared to participate in constitutional government for some years, I know of no arrangement so proper for them as territorial governments. There they can learn the principles of freedom and eat the fruit of foul rebellion..."[81]

In that session, the Thirteenth Amendment to the Constitution, abolishing slavery (without compensation to the owners), was ratified by the States. The Fourteenth Amendment was then proposed over President Johnson's veto. This would bar all supporters of the Confederacy from Federal and State offices, and require the Southern States to repudiate their war debt but share in the payment of the Union war debt. Tennessee ratified, but the ten ex-Confederate States that rejected it lost their identities in March of 1867 with the passage by Congress of the First Reconstruction Act:[82]

"WHEREAS no legal State governments or adequate protection for life or property now exists in the rebel States of Virginia, North Carolina, South Carolina, Georgia, Mississippi, Alabama, Louisiana, Florida, Texas, and Arkansas; and whereas it is necessary that peace and good order should be enforced in said States until loyalty and republican State governments can be legally established: Therefore

"*Be it enacted* ... That said rebel States shall be divided into military districts and made subject to the military authority of the United States, as hereinafter prescribed, and for that purpose Virginia shall constitute the first district; North Carolina and South Carolina the second district; Georgia, Alabama, and Florida, the third district; Mississippi and Arkansas the fourth district; and Louisiana and Texas the fifth district....

"When the people of any one of said rebel States shall have formed a constitution of government in conformity with the Constitution of the United States in all respects, framed by a convention of delegates elected by the male citizens of said State twenty-one years old and upward, of whatever race, color, or previous condition, who have been resident of that State for one year previous to the day of such election, except such as may be disfranchised for participation in the rebellion ... and when said State, by a vote of its legislature elected under said constitution, shall have adopted the amendment to the Constitution of the United States, proposed by the thirty-ninth Congress, and known as article fourteen, and when said article shall have become a part of the Constitution of the United States, said State shall be declared entitled to representation in Congress...."[83]

It might be asked that if these States were out of the Union and under martial law, how could they ratify an amendment to the Constitution of a Union they were not in, and if they were in the Union, how could they be compelled to ratify it? The answer, of course, is Federal bayonets. The voluntary compact of sovereign States created by the Founders was being purposely "Reconstructed" by a murderous and unconstitutional usurpation of power into a coerced Yankee Empire.

Strangers and unscrupulous adventurers from the North, often with their entire worldly possessions carried in a carpetbag, came flocking into the South with the Freedmen's Bureau and the Union League to pick over the bones like buzzards. The Freedmen's Bureau was an agency whose purpose was to help the Blacks adjust to the new order. Many in the Bureau were honest and charitable, while others were corrupt; but it was the Union League that had the real influence in organizing the Blacks for Radical purposes. The Union League was formed in the dark days during the war to revive the failing spirits of the Northern people. After the war, emissaries of the League flocked to the South to organize the Blacks and turn them into good voting Radicals. As Claude Bowers wrote in his work *The Tragic Era,* "Left to themselves, the negroes would have turned for leadership to the native whites, who understood them best. This was the danger. Imperative, then, that they should be taught to hate—and teachers of hate were plentiful..."[84]

Walter Fleming described the work of the Union League: "It was one of the first organizations to declare for negro suffrage and the disfranchisement of Confederates; it held steadily to this declaration during the four years following the war; and it continued as a sort of bureau in the radical Republican party for the purpose of controlling the negro vote in the South.... By the spring of 1866, the negroes were widely organized under this leadership, and it needed but slight change to convert the negro meetings into local councils of the Union League... Over the South went the organizers, until by 1868 the last negroes were gathered into the fold....

The influence of the League over the negro was due in large degree to the mysterious secrecy of the meetings, the weird initiation ceremony that made him feel fearfully good from his head to his heels, the imposing ritual, and the songs. The ritual, it is said, was not used in the North; it was probably adopted for the particular benefit of the African... He was told to the accompaniment of clanking chains and groans that the objects of the order were to preserve liberty, to perpetuate the Union, to maintain the laws and the Constitution, to secure the ascendancy of American institutions, to protect, defend, and strengthen all loyal men and members of the Union League... The council then sang *Hail, Columbia!* and *The Star Spangled Banner*, after which an official lectured the candidates, saying that though the designs of traitors had been thwarted, there were yet to be secured legislative triumphs and the complete ascendancy of the true principles of popular government, equal liberty, education and elevation of the workmen, and the overthrow at the ballot box of the old oligarchy of political leaders. After prayer by the chaplain, the room was darkened, alcohol on salt flared up with a ghastly light as the 'fire of liberty,' and the members joined hands in a circle around the candidate, who was made to place one hand on the flag and, with the other raised, swear again to support the government and to elect true Union men to office... White men who joined the order before the negroes were admitted and who left when the latter became members asserted that the negroes were taught in these meetings that the only way to have peace and plenty, to get 'the forty acres and a mule,' was to kill some of the leading whites in each community as a warning to others. In North Carolina twenty-eight barns were burned in one county by negroes who believed that Governor Holden, the head of the State League, had ordered it... That outrages were comparatively few was due, not to any sensible teachings of the leaders, but to the fundamental good nature of the blacks... The relations between the races, indeed, continued on the whole to be friendly until 1867–68... With the organization of the League, the negroes grew more reserved, and finally became openly unfriendly to the whites..."[85] To further cement power, the Blacks were compelled to join the Union League Militia to keep any Conservative Blacks in line, and to intimidate the Whites. [86]

Radical Republican plans were well-laid for control of Virginia: The Freedmen's Bureau, Union League, and office-holding carpet-baggers would deliver the Black vote, while the Federal Army of Occupation would correct any slips. Two notorious Radicals were the carpetbagger Judge John C. Underwood and the scalawag Reverend James W. Hunnicut. Underwood included Blacks on a Virginia jury for the first time, and delivered an inflammatory address to them accusing Confederates of being motivated by the "fiery soul of treason" and deliberately murdering Federal Prisoners of War by starvation, yellow fever, and smallpox. Hunnicut operated a Radical newspaper in Richmond after the war in which he told the Blacks: "The white race have houses and lands. Some of you are old and feeble and cannot carry the musket but can apply the torch to the dwelling of your enemies. There are none too young— the boy of ten and the girl of twelve can apply the torch".[87]

Robert Somers, an English visitor to the South five years after the war, describes the upheaval wrought by Reconstruction and the Union League: "The negroes, after the Confederate surrender, were disorderly. Many of them would not settle down to labour on any terms, but roamed about with arms in their hands and hunger in their bellies; and the governing power, with the usual blind determination of a victorious party, was thinking only all the while of every device of suffrage and reconstruction by which 'the freedmen' might be strengthened, and made, under Northern dictation, the ruling power in the country. Agitators of the loosest fiber came down among the towns and plantations, and organizing a Union league, held midnight meetings with the negroes in the woods, and went about uttering sentiments which, to say the least, in all the circumstances were anti-social and destructive. Crimes and outrages increased. The law, which must be always more or less weak in all thinly populated countries, was all but powerless; and the new Governments in the South, supposing them to have been most willing, were certainly unable to repress disorder, or to spread a general sense of security throughout the community. A real terror reigned for a time among the white people; and in this situation the 'Ku-Klux' started into being. It was one of those secret organizations which spring up in disordered states of society, when the bonds of law and government are all but dissolved, and when no confidence is felt in the regular public administration of justice. But the power with which the 'Ku-Klux' moved in many parts of the South, the knowledge it displayed of all that was going on, the fidelity with which its secret was kept, and the complacency with which it was regarded by the general community, gave this mysterious body a prominence and importance seldom attained by such illegal and deplorable associations. Nearly every respectable man in the Southern States was not only disfranchised, but under fear of arrest or confiscation; the old foundations of authority were utterly razed before any new ones had yet been laid, and in the dark and benighted interval the remains of the Confederate armies—swept, after a long and heroic day of fair fight, from the field—flitted before the eye of the people in this weird and midnight shape of a 'Ku-Klux-Klan'".[88] As a result, harsh new Federal "force" laws were enacted, usurping the power of state courts, and enabling the Federal Government to enforce the provisions of the Fourteenth Amendment, even though evidence showed that the Klan arose as a result of Union League brutality, and its corrupt and criminal activities.[89]

In October 1867, the eligible voters of Virginia, or "Military District Number One," elected delegates to a Constitutional Convention. Of the 102 delegates seated, 32 were Conservatives and 70 were Radicals. Of the Radicals, 25 were Black, 6 were from foreign countries, and the rest were carpetbaggers or scalawags. Judge Underwood presided, and therefore it was known as "The Underwood Convention." It met in Richmond in December of 1867.[90]

A letter written by Joseph A. Waddell, a Conservative member of the Convention representing Augusta County, gave a description of the body: "The white Radicals are a motley crew. Some of them have apparently little more intelligence than the negroes, and have doubtless come from the lowest ranks of the people. The leaders, with three or four exceptions, are Northern men who came to this State with the Federal army in the capacity of petty officers, chaplains, commissaries, clerks, sutlers, etc. Others were probably employees of the Freedmen's Bureau, and when that institution dispensed with their services were left here stranded like frogs in a dried-up mill-pond. Having no other resource they plunged into politics. They are now jubilant in the receipt of eight dollars a day from the treasury of the State, and happy in anticipation of the fat offices they are to get by means of the same voters who sent them to the Convention. In regard to the latter particular, however, they may be disappointed. The negroes have their eyes on the same places for themselves, and will probably claim them... The Radical members of the Convention were of course elected by the votes of negroes, the whites yielding to apathy in many counties where it might have been otherwise. Some of the Northern leaders were men of good talent, but all were, more or less, possessed by a spirit of vindictive hostility to everything distinctively Virginian, and sought to frame all the institutions of the State according to the New England pattern"[91].

In a description of the proceedings of the 29th of January 1868, Waddell states: "I have a suspicion that some of the white Radicals are getting sick of their black allies. The white leaders expected the blacks to be a very tractable set of voters, so excessively in love with 'the old flag,' and so thoroughly 'loyal,' as to give all the good fat places to the pale-faces. But genius will assert itself,—the star of Africa is in the ascendant, and the light of its civilization is dawning upon us. The new era, beginning with 'equality before the law,' has now reached the stage of 'manhood suffrage,' and the consummation of no distinction *anywhere* 'on account of race or color' is hastening on. No, not exactly that,—there is to be distinction, for the blacks seem to claim the honors and emoluments without bearing the burdens of government. The black speakers scold and hector their white associates, whom they suspect of an indisposition to toe the mark. Some of the latter cower and cajole, and do everything possible to conciliate. Others of the whites, however, are evidently restive. They have caught a Tartar."[92]

Eventually, and one-by-one, the Southern States—under carpetbag governments, "Black and Tan" conventions, and Federal bayonets—created and ratified Radical Constitutions that met with the approval of the Yankees, the Fourteenth Amendment was ratified, and the States (*in* the Union for purposes of rule and plunder but *out of* the Union for any recourse to Constitutional rights) were "re-admitted" to the Union and representation in Congress. With the South subjugated and the voluntary Union of sovereign States thus transformed into a coerced Empire "pinned together by bayonets," and with its politics along with its finances under the total control of the North, the Yankees went away to deal with the Indians of the Western Plains, who were in the way of their trans-continental railways, leaving their Black puppets to the upheaval they had wrought in Southern society; but leaving also, as a legacy of their corruption, a bloc of voters readily malleable in the hands of the Party of Big Government however that government might be ruled, whether by a despot, an oligarchy, or a democratic mob under the sway of demagogues.

VIII.

Up From Slavery And Back Again

And what is debt? In an individual, it is slavery.
It is slavery of the worst sort, surpassing
that of the West India Islands, for it enslaves
the mind as well as it enslaves the body...

—John Randolph of Roanoke[93]

"LIBERTY, EQUALITY, FRATERNITY!" has come down to us as the lofty rallying-cry of the French Revolution, but in Charles Dickens' classic *A Tale of Two Cities,* it is rendered as *"Liberty, Equality, Fraternity or Death!"*[94] and we all know of the guillotine and its work. But Liberty and Equality are mutually exclusive and inversely proportional to one another in any government, and true Fraternity—an impulse welling up from within the individual towards his fellow man—cannot be imposed from without; therefore the French Revolution's march towards *Liberty, Equality, Fraternity or Death* proved to be a march towards the perfect *Equality* of slavery to a totalitarian government devoid of all *Liberty,* and a coerced, affected *Fraternity* cowering in the shadow of the guillotine.

The French Revolution destroyed the aristocracy, but the basic dichotomy remained, with the aristocracy merely replaced by the bourgeoisie. The same happened here after Lincoln's War, with the agrarian patricians of the old Republic merely replaced by a capitalist and mercantile oligarchy; while agrarian slaves were replaced by industrial wage workers, and slave insurrections were replaced by labor strife and urban riots. The Russian Revolution played it out again, when the Tsarist autocracy was replaced by the Bolshevik Party, and the peasants were herded off the land and into a forced industrial "workers' paradise" through government orchestrated famines and re-education camps. "Life has become better, comrades. Life has become more joyous," declared Stalin[95] just before the bloody purges and deportations to the Siberian gulags during "The Great Terror" in the 1930s.

Is this where the "woke" Progressives are taking us, with their Fascist ANTIFA rent-a-thugs, their Marxist Black Lives Matter mobs, their Anti-White and Anti-West Critical Race Theories, and their hubristic claims of being on "the right side of history"? History is cyclic, not linear, so there is no such thing as "the right side of history," and the cycles of history abundantly show that Utopian dreams inevitably turn into totalitarian nightmares. Perhaps, then, we may learn something from the Cyclic March of History by looking at the French Revolution, Lincoln's Revolution, and the Russian Revolution—and then look at the "Woke Revolution" of today to see if there is any connection. Follow the dollar and know the truth.

As Napoleon said, "Money has no motherland; financiers are without patriotism and without decency: their sole object is gain".[96] The first global financial network in modern times was founded by the House of Rothschild, attaining great success by the end of the eighteenth century by lending money on interest to governments and kings, and parlaying wealth into political power. Wars are profitable to bankers because they expand the debts of the antagonists. If an antagonist doesn't exist, then one must be created by financing the rise of a hostile regime. While the virtues of peace must always be proclaimed; perpetual conflict is where the money is. Both sides of the conflict may be financed, giving them each a 50/50 chance to win, but giving a one hundred percent chance for the global bankers to win. If a government does not wish to borrow money to finance the conflict, then it would be necessary to encourage a revolution to replace it with one that does. G. Edward Griffin calls this "The Rothschild Formula",[97] and its footprints may be found on the three revolutions looked at here—and on the "Woke Revolution" today.

King Louis XVI of France inherited large French debts. His policy of taking out international loans rather than increasing taxes further increased the debt, while his helping to finance the American Revolution brought France near to bankruptcy.[98] That, combined with poor harvests and bread shortages, sparked the French Revolution. In 1789, the king was deposed, and the revolutionary government took over. European bankers would not risk any large loans to it as long as there was the possibility that the king could return and repudiate the debts, so Louis XVI was offered a cumbersome coach in which to "escape" to Austria. He was captured at the border, returned under guard, condemned to die for treason, and beheaded in 1793. His queen, Marie Antoinette, was beheaded thereafter. The international bankers foreclosed on Louis XVI's France, and made safe new loans to the revolution.[99]

In the middle of the nineteenth century, the Wall Street Money Trust ginned up sectional hatred in America by helping to finance the publication of *Uncle Tom's Cabin*, the repeal of the Missouri Compromise, the case of *Dred Scott*, the issue of slavery in the Territories, "Bleeding Kansas," Abolitionist terrorism, and John Brown's Raid, which finally drove the South to secession, lit the fuse to Lincoln's War,[100] and inaugurated massive Union indebtedness to Wall Street. After the conquest of the Southern States, Confederate President Jefferson Davis was to be hanged by military tribunal for treason (more out of vindictive hatred for the South than to prevent him from coming back into power and repudiating the debts of the "carpetbagger" governments and their Black puppets who now ruled the Southern States. The assassination of Lincoln did more to benefit the plunderers of the South than the hanging of Jefferson Davis ever would have.) However, with the return of the civil courts, the Federal Government never tried Davis for treason for fear of his being declared not guilty and thereby losing in court what was won by the war.[101] But the South was still prostrate under the iron heel of Reconstruction, and while the Southern Whites were kept at bayonet-point, the carpetbag governments ratified the Fourteenth Amendment to the Constitution, which gutted the Tenth Amendment and State sovereignty, and—among other things—forced the conquered South to pay for the Union war debts and repudiate her own.[102] This, along with her total devastation from the war and the plunder of her resources then and thereafter, kept the South in poverty until the Second World War, while Wall Street and the Money Trust gamboled in the Gilded Age.[103]

Russia freed her serfs in 1861. The Tsar gave them land to purchase and forty-nine years to pay for it. But depression hit, followed by Russia's unsuccessful Russo-Japanese War in 1904–5. The peasants couldn't pay their mortgages, pay their taxes, pay for the war, and feed their families all at the same time, so they revolted in 1905. The Tsar was both the Government and the Church, and therefore, owned the lands of both. He was heavily in debt to the international bankers, with much land as collateral, but there was no way for the bankers to foreclose as long as the Tsar had an army. A revolution was the ticket. The seeds had already been sown with the revolt of 1905, and fertilized with Marxist propaganda. In 1914, as a result of the Austria-Serbia crisis on his border, Tsar Nicolas II mobilized his army. This hopefully would both avoid revolution and give him the excuse to borrow more money to relieve the suffering population. But Germany saw the mobilization as an act of war and declared war on Russia as Europe descended into the First World War. Russia's peasant army was no match for the most powerful army on earth, and when Russia suffered a reverse, the troops mutinied, killed their officers, and headed for home. The Russian front collapsed, Tsar Nicolas II was told his government was ended, and the Communists took over with the October Revolution of 1917. To ensure the Tsar could not return to power and repudiate the loans made to the Communists, he and his family were executed. The bankers then foreclosed on Tsarist Russia, and made safe new loans to the Communists.[104]

To ask what these revolutions and "The Rothschild Formula" have to do with the "Woke Revolution" today, a look at our national debt approaching thirty-six trillion dollars should first give one pause. Bankers are creditors who make big money off of loans, so it is good business for bankers—who are among the most fiscally conservative people on earth—to promote profligacy, irresponsibility, and dependency among potential debtors. If war is where the money is in the international arena, at home the ticket is the Welfare State—or Socialism, or Communism, or whatever other iterations of collective dependency on government handouts you may choose—for it increases government borrowing to pay for it. Therefore, politicians who promise more government handouts (both to citizens and to corporations) have been promoted by the Money Trust and Wall Street ever since the Lincoln Administration sold out the financial independence of the United States Government with the Second National Bank Act of 1863. America is now a debtor in the grip of Morgan, Rothschild, and their affiliates on Wall Street—a grip which tightened with the Federal Reserve Act of 1913[105]—and to challenge them is futile. As John Randolph of Roanoke said of National Banks long ago, "You might as well attack Gibraltar with a pocket pistol as to attempt to punish them."[106]

The Welfare State not only increases the national debt, it also creates political opposition, and as stated in "The Rothschild Formula," Wall Street bankers have no qualms about financing both sides of any conflict. However, the side that promises the most expansion of the Welfare State is the side that bankers will find more profitable, so that is the side to bet on. In addition to the Welfare State there are other ways for Wall Street to profit domestically. Radical "human rights" policies, "civil rights" policies, and "affirmative action" policies of government that presume to correct the deficiencies in God's Creation require an ever-expanding bureaucracy to administer them. This increases the size of government, which also increases borrowing to pay for it (if the political inexpediency of raising taxes is to be avoided.) Therefore, Wall Street will always promote the radical politicians and the radical media who promote these government-expanding policies.

What, then, are the policies of the "Woke Revolution" today, and how do the Money Powers fit in? The Republic of Sovereign States founded in 1788 was violently usurped by Lincoln's War and "Reconstructed" into an Empire pinned together by bayonets. Following Polybius' Cyclic March of History, the Empire's democratic gloss has devolved into an ochlocracy orchestrated by the

Money Powers and their political demagogues through the use of universal suffrage, control of the media, and the twisting of the Constitution into a "living document." Pandering to the mob and its baser appetites, demagogues grovel ever deeper into the mire for ignorant votes, undermining personal responsibility with ever-expanding "civil rights," "affirmative actions," and government "entitlements"—all of which increase and expand the government bureaucracies to implement and administer them, and increase the government indebtedness to the Money Powers to pay for them. Meanwhile—using the same "divide and rule" tactics of the Union Leagues and the carpetbaggers during Reconstruction—these demagogues stir up hatred by creating a revolutionary coalition of constituents (known in this case as "intersectionality") among the ever-growing non-White population, radical feminists, homosexuals, transgenders, and other non-traditionalists by preaching anti-West and anti-White Critical Race Theory, and replacing the traditional Marxist class conflict with a neo-Marxist race conflict between the "cisgender White oppressors" and everyone else. In addition to "reparations" and other shakedowns of the Whites, their demands are for Western Civilization to repudiate its heritage—from the Greek philosophers to the American Founders—for the sake of Equity with those who have none, and to "take a knee" to the eternal Marxist present. To effect this requires a totalitarian government.

As the Welfare State is in debt thirty-six trillion dollars to the Federal Reserve bankers, it appears now that the Money Powers—in their latest iteration of "The Rothschild Formula"—are fertilizing the seeds of a totalitarian revolution, just as when they foreclosed on the deeply indebted Tsar Nicholas II of Russia with the Bolshevik Revolution in 1917. Hannah Arendt, in her classic work *The Origins of Totalitarianism*, said that "Equality of condition among their subjects has been one of the foremost concerns of despotisms and tyrannies since ancient times, yet such equalization is not sufficient for totalitarian rule because it leaves more or less intact certain nonpolitical communal bonds between the subjects, such as family ties and communal cultural interests...

Totalitarian movements are mass organizations of atomized, isolated individuals".[107]

The Bolsheviks and Stalinists of the Soviet Union succeeded superbly in creating such an organization by destroying families and civil society, and isolating neighbors, friends, and family members from each other by having them bear false witness against each other to the Secret Police through fear of the gulag. Such blatant brutality is not suitable for an "open" society, however, so more discrete methods are called for, using the techniques of persuasion long used in marketing and political demagoguery. Of such is the push for the implementation of "Diversity, Equity, and Inclusion" (DEI) which would level society by decree, backed by the threats and powers of the State. But that alone is not sufficient for totalitarian rule, because it leaves intact civil society (family, religion, and private life and organizations) which then must be undermined with a "Long March" by a leftist academia, media, and judiciary to reduce individuals to cyphers totally dependent upon a centralized, totalitarian government.

As the Welfare State absolves fathers of their parental duties, takes children's education away from parental oversight, and glorifies, celebrates and codifies into law "free love," "no-fault divorce," abortion, sodomy, transgenderism and other sexual deviancies as "civil rights," it further undermines the family by paying single women (mostly in the urban Black housing projects) to indiscriminately breed a growing horde of revolutionaries, and then feeds, clothes, and houses them at government expense while indoctrinating them with Critical Race Theory in the government schools.[108] When the cost of servicing the metastasizing national debt that is paying for all this exceeds the income available, and when more printed government bonds sold for more printed money make these Socialist welfare "entitlements" worthless with inflation, the moment will have arrived to foreclose on Western Civilization with the threat of a race war to hang like a Sword of Damocles over the body politic to effect the consummation of this totalitarian "Woke Revolution."

The first to "take a knee" to the "wokelings," of course, would be the guilt-ridden Desperate White Liberals who would—in their final and supreme self-immolating act of virtue-signaling—interbreed themselves out of existence. For those "enemies of the people" who would have the audacity to resist, there would be ANTIFA and Black Lives Matter "social justice warriors" to "re-educate" them. And for those unreconstructed sinners who refuse to "take a knee" to the "wokelings," and who are not beholding to the Money Trust for anything and thus present a mortal threat to the Deep State, there would be disarmament by "red flag" laws, the freezing of assets, and "lawfare"—with Madame Defarge sitting in the jury box knitting shrouds for the accused.

Results? The "shadow line" will have been crossed whereby the government is no longer the servant of the citizens, as was intended by the Founders long ago, but the citizens are now the servants of the government, which history has abundantly shown to be the end goal of Marxists and all other despots everywhere, and which is the end goal of the Woke Revolution. As ever, the basic dichotomy will remain; only the Utopian nightmare will have changed—this time with the enslavement of merit[109] to carry the DEI deadwood of a totalitarian bureaucracy[110] surrounded by a wall of skulls, while Wall Street and the global Money Powers—beaming benignantly down upon it all—count the blood money.

Afterword

The Gods of The Copybook Headings
By Rudyard Kipling[111]

As I pass through my incarnations in every age
and race,

I make my proper prostrations to the Gods of the
Market-Place.

Peering through reverent fingers I watch them
flourish and fall,

And the Gods of the Copybook Headings, I notice,
outlast them all.

We were living in trees when they met us. They
showed us each in turn

That Water would certainly wet us, as Fire would
certainly burn:

But we found them lacking in Uplift, Vision and
Breadth of Mind,

So we left them to teach the Gorillas while we
followed the March of Mankind.

We moved as the Spirit listed. *They* never altered
their pace,

Being neither cloud nor wind-borne like the Gods
of the Market-Place;

But they always caught up with our progress, and
    presently word would come

That a tribe had been wiped off its icefield, or the
    lights had gone out in Rome.

With the Hopes that our World is built on they
    were utterly out of touch.

They denied that the Moon was Stilton; they
    denied she was even Dutch.

They denied that Wishes were Horses; they denied
    that a Pig had Wings.

So we worshipped the Gods of the Market Who
    promised these beautiful things.

When the Cambrian measures were forming, They
    promised perpetual peace.

They swore, if we gave them our weapons, that the
    wars of the tribes would cease.

But when we disarmed They sold us and delivered
    us bound to our foe,

And the Gods of the Copybook Headings said:
    "Stick to the Devil you know."

On the first Feminian Sandstones we were prom-
    ised the Fuller Life

(Which started by loving our neighbor and ended
    by loving his wife)

Till our women had no more children and the men
    lost reason and faith,

And the Gods of the Copybook Headings said:
    "The Wages of Sin is Death."

In the Carboniferous Epoch we were promised
    abundance for all,

By robbing selected Peter to pay for collective Paul;

But, though we had plenty of money, there was nothing our money could buy,

And the Gods of the Copybook Headings said: *"If you don't work you die."*

Then the Gods of the Market tumbled, and their smooth-tongued wizards withdrew,

And the hearts of the meanest were humbled and began to believe it was true

That all is not Gold that Glitters, and Two and Two make Four –

And the gods of the Copybook Headings limped up to explain it once more:

As it will be in the future, it was at the birth of Man –

There are only four things certain since Social Progress began:

That the Dog returns to his Vomit and the Sow returns to her Mire,

And the burnt Fool's bandaged finger goes wabbling back to the fire;

And that after this is accomplished, and the brave new world begins

When all men are paid for existing and no man must pay for his sins,

As surely as Water will wet us, as surely as Fire will burn,

The Gods of the Copybook Headings with terror and slaughter return.

Endnotes

1   Allen Tate, "Aeneas at Washington" in *Collected Poems 1919-1976*, Paperback ed. (New York: Farrar Straus Giroux, 2007) pg. 69.

2   Admiral Raphael Semmes, CSN, *Memoirs of Service Afloat During the War Between the States* (1868; Baton Rouge and London: Louisiana State UP, 1996) pg. 293.

3   *Ibid*, pgs. 53-5.

4   Alfred, Lord Tennyson, "Merlin and Vivien," in *Idylls of the King* (1892; New York: Airmont Publishing Co, 1969) pg. 166.

5   Thomas Carlyle, *Latter-day Pamphlets*, "IV: The New Downing Street," in *The Works of Thomas Carlyle*, 12 vols. Library ed. (New York: John B. Alden, 1885) Vol. 8.

6   Sir Winston Churchill, *A History of the English Speaking Peoples*, 4 vols. (New York: Dodd, Mead & Co., 1958) 4: 170-3.

7   1790 U.S. Census, in Thomas Prentiss Kettell, *Southern Wealth and Northern Profits* (New York: George W. & John A. Wood, 1860) pg. 120.

8   Abraham Lincoln, "First Inaugural Address" (1861), in Charles W. Eliot, ed, *The Harvard Classics*. 50 vols. (New York: P. F. Collier & Son, 1910) Vol. 43, *American Historical Documents*, pgs. 334-6.

9   Alexis de Tocqueville, *Democracy in America*, 2 vols. Trans. Henry Reeve (New York: D. Appleton, 1904) The Henry Reeve text as revised by Francis Bowen (New York: Vantage Books, 1954) 1: 381-2.

10   Abraham Lincoln, "Emancipation Proclamation" (1863), in Eliot, 43: 344-6.

11   Lerone Bennett, Jr., *Forced into Glory: Abraham Lincoln's White Dream* (Chicago: Johnson Publishing Co., 2000) pgs. 183-214.

12   Abraham Lincoln, "Second Inaugural Address (1865), in Eliot, 43: 451.

13   *Ibid,* "First Inaugural Address" (1861), in Eliot, 43: 336-7.

14   Gene Kizer, Jr., *Slavery Was Not the Cause of the War Between the States: The Irrefutable Argument* (Charleston and James Island, S.C.: Charleston Athenaeum Press, 2014) pgs. 56-69.

15   Charles W. Ramsdell, "Lincoln and Ft. Sumter," *The Journal of Southern History*, Vol. 3, Issue 3 (August 1937) pgs. 259-88, in Kizer, pgs. 197-248. See also John Shipley Tilley, *Lincoln Takes Command* (Chapel Hill: UNC P., 1941) pgs. 179-87, 266-7, 306-12, with documentation from original sources, including the *Official Records*

16   Tocqueville, 2: 425.

17   Gov. John Letcher, letter to Sec. Simon Cameron, April 16, 1861, in the Richmond *Enquirer*, April 18, 1861, pg. 2, col. 1. Microfilm. The Daily Richmond *Enquirer*, Jan. 1, 1861—June 29, 1861. Film 23, reel 24 (Richmond: Library of Virginia collection).

18   "Lee's Farewell to His Army," April 10, 1865, in Eliot, 43: 449.

19   Thaddeus Stevens, "The Conquered Provinces," *Congressional Globe*, December 18, 1865, 72, in Walter L. Fleming, ed. *Documentary History of Reconstruction: Political, Military, Social, Religious, Educational and Industrial, 1865 to 1906*, 2 vols. (Cleveland: The Arthur H. Clark Co., 1906) 1: 148.

20   *Acts and Resolutions, 39 Cong., 2 sess.*, 60, in Fleming, ed. *Documentary History*, 1: 401-3.

21   Jim Downs, *Sick from Freedom: African-American Illness and Suffering During the Civil War and Reconstruction* (Oxford: Oxford UP, 2012) *passim*. See also John Remington Graham, *The American Civil War as a Crusade to Free the Slaves* (South Boston, VA: Gerald C. Burnett, 2016) pgs. 10-3.

22   Henry E. Vanden and Gary Prevost, *The Politics of Latin America: The Power Game.* (Oxford: Oxford UP, 2002) pgs. 153-4, 156-60.

23   Thomas Prentiss Kettell, *Southern Wealth and Northern Profits* (New York: 1860) p. 19.

24   Tocqueville, 2: 425.

25   *Journal of the House of Delegates of the State of Virginia for the Extra Session, 1861* (Richmond: William F. Ritchie, Public Printer, 1861) pgs. 9-10 (to be found in the Special Collection of the Library of Virginia.) *Official Records of the Union and Confederate Navies in the War of the Rebellion.*

26 *Official Records of the Union and Confederate Navies in the War of the Rebellion.* (31 vols. Washington, 1894-1927) ser. 1, Vol. 4, pg. 251; see also Tilley, pgs. 266-7.

27 Churchill, 4: 169.

28 Carlyle, "Latter-day Pamphlets IV: The New Downing Street," in *Works*, Vol. 8.

29 "The Declaration of Independence" (1776). Eliot, 43: 160-1.

30 Virginia Commission on Constitutional Government, *We the States: An Anthology of Historic Documents and Commentaries thereon, Expounding the State and Federal Relationship* (Richmond: The Wm. Byrd P, 1964) pgs. 70-1.

31 *Ibid*, pgs. 75-6.

32 Charles Adams, *When in the Course of Human Events: Arguing the Case for Southern Secession* (Lanham. Boulder. New York. Oxford: Rowman & Littlefield Publishers, Inc., 2000) pgs. 14-6.

33 Thomas J. DiLorenzo, *The Problem with Lincoln* (Washington DC: Regnery History, 2020) pgs. 75-93.

34 Thomas Jefferson to William Charles Jarvis, Sept. 28, 1820, in *We the States*, pg. 258.

35 Philip Leigh, *Southern Reconstruction* (Yardley, PA: Westholme Publishing, 2017) pg. 52.

36 Adams, pg. 66.

37 John Remington Graham, *Blood Money: The Civil War and the Federal Reserve* (Gretna: Pelican Publishing Co., 2012) pgs. 60-4. Also, G. Edward Griffin, *The Creature from Jekyll Island: A Second Look at the Federal Reserve*, 4th ed. (1994; Westlake Village, CA: American Media, 2002) pgs. 384-6.

38 Graham, *Blood Money*, pgs. 29-50.

39 Kizer, pgs. 35-7, 199-248.

40 Graham, *Blood Money*, pgs. 51-2.

41 Adams, pgs. 177-80.

42 Graham, *Blood Money*, pgs. 64-6.

43 *Ibid*, pgs. 66-7.

44 Thomas Jefferson, "The Kentucky Resolutions," in *We the States*, pgs. 143-4.

45 Abraham Lincoln, "First Inaugural Address," (1861). Eliot, 43: 334.

46 *Ibid*, "Emancipation Proclamation," (1863), Eliot, 43: 345.

47 Brian Purnell and Jeanne Theoharis, Eds., with Komozi Woodard, *The Strange Careers of the Jim Crow North: Segregation and Struggle outside of the South* (New York: New York UP, 2019) pgs. 13-7. See also Thomas J. DiLorenzo, *The Real Lincoln: A New Look at Abraham Lincoln, His Agenda, and an Unnecessary War* (New York: Three Rivers P, 2003) pgs. 24-8.

48 DiLorenzo, *The Real Lincoln*, pgs. 21-4.

49 Bennett, pgs. 183-214.

50 DiLorenzo, *The Real Lincoln*, pgs. 16-20.

51 Zora Neale Hurston, *Barracoon: The Story of the Last "Black Cargo."* Ed. Deborah G. Plant (New York: Amistad/Harper Collins, 2018) pgs. 9-10.

52 Dr. Carter G. Woodson, PhD, *Free Negro Owners of Slaves in the United States in 1830, Together with Absentee Ownership of Slaves in the United States in 1830* (Washington, DC: The Association for the Study of Negro Life and History, 1924) pgs. 1-42.

53 Zora Neale Hurston, *Dust Tracks on a Road: An Autobiography.* 2nd ed. (1942; Urbanna: U of Illinois P, 1984) pg. 84. See also Hurston, *Barracoon, passim.*

54 Woodson, pgs. i-viii, 1-42.

55 Maj. Heros von Borcke, CSA, *Memoirs of the Confederate War for Independence.* (Philadelphia: J. B. Lippincott & Co., 1867) pg. 182.

56 Rudyard Kipling, "The White Man's Burden" (1899). *Rudyard Kipling's Verse.* Inclusive ed. (Garden City & New York: Doubleday, Page & Co., 1919) pg. 372.

57 Prof. Robert Lewis Dabney, D.D. *A Defense of Virginia (And Through Her, of the South) in the Recent and Pending Contests against the Sectional Party* (New York: E. J. Hale & Son, 1867) pgs. 27-31. (Reprinted by Sprinkle Publications, Harrisonburg, VA, 1977.)

58 *Ibid.*, pgs. 33-41.

59 DuBois, Pg. 179.

60 Virginia History and Government Textbook Commission, *Cavalier Commonwealth—History and Government of Virginia* (New York: McGraw-Hill, 1957) pgs. 119, 161.

61 Dabney, pg. 43.

62 William Cabell Bruce, *John Randolph of Roanoke 1773-1833*. 2 vols. (New York & London: The Knickerbocker P, 1922) 2: 203.

63 Edward A. Pollard, *Southern History of the War*. 2 vols. (New York: Charles B. Richardson, 1866) 2: 198.

64 William Faulkner, *The Unvanquished* (1938; New York: Vintage/ Random House, 1991) pgs. 91-2.

65 Shelby Foote, *The Civil War: A Narrative*. 3 vols. (1974; New York: Vintage/Random House, 1986) 3: 649.

66 Pollard, pgs. 198-9.

67 *Ibid*, pg. 199.

68 *Ibid*, pgs. 201-2.

69 Otto Eisenschiml, *Why Was Lincoln Murdered?* (1937; London: Forgotten Books—Classic Reprint Series, 2018) pgs. 309-11, 366-8, 427-8.

70 George Fitzhugh, *Cannibals All! or Slaves Without Masters* (1857; Cambridge: The Belknap P of Harvard UP, 1960) pgs. 15-20, "The Universal Trade."

71 "Lincoln's Gettysburg Address" (1863), Eliot 43: 441.

72 "Emancipation Proclamation" (1863), Eliot 43: 344-6.

73 Virginia Museum of History and Culture: "The Cult of the Lost Cause." https://www.virginiahistory.org/what-you-can-see/story-virginia/ explore-story-virginia/1861-1876/reconstruction.

74 Paul Kennedy, *The Rise and Fall of the Great Powers* (New York: Vintage/Random House, 1989) pgs. 178-82.

75 Foote, 3: 729.

76 "Lee's Farewell to His Army" (1865), Eliot 43: 449.

77 Lt. E. M. Boykin, *The Falling Flag* (New York: E. J. Hale & Son, 1874) pgs. 64-7.

78 Churchill, 4: 172-3.

79 *Cavalier Commonwealth*, pgs. 337-40, 346.

80 *Ibid*, pg. 347.

81 Thaddeus Stevens, "The Conquered Provinces," *Congressional Globe*, December 18, 1865, 72, in Fleming, ed., *Documentary History*, 1: 148.

82   *Cavalier Commonwealth*, pgs. 346-8.

83   *Acts and Resolutions, 39 Cong., 2 Sess.*, 60, in Fleming, ed., *Documentary History*, 1: 401-3.

84   Claude Bowers, *The Tragic Era: The Revolution after Lincoln* (Cambridge: The Riverside P, 1929) pg. 198.

85   Walter L. Fleming, ed. *The Sequel of Appomattox: A Chronicle of the Reunion of the States*. Textbook Ed. The Chronicles of America Series. Ed. Allen Johnson. Gerhard R. Lomer and Charles W. Jeffreys, assistant eds. (New Haven: Yale OP, 1919) pgs. 178-88.

86   John Chodes, *Washington's KKK: The Union League during Southern Reconstruction* (Columbia, S.C.: Shotwell Publishing, 2016) pg. 33.

87   *Cavalier Commonwealth*, pgs. 349-50.

88   Robert Somers, *The Southern States since the War 1870-1* (London and New York: MacMillan and Co., 1871) pgs. 153-4.

89   Chodes, pg. 47.

90   *Cavalier Commonwealth*, pg. 351.

91   Jos. A. Waddell, *Annals of Augusta County, Virginia, from 1726 to 1871*. 2nd ed. revised (Staunton: C. Russell Caldwell, 1902) pgs. 515-22.

92   *Ibid*, pgs. 515-22.

93   John Randolph of Roanoke, Speech on the Greek Cause, January 24, 1824, quoted in Russell Kirk, *John Randolph of Roanoke: A Study in American Politics*, 4th ed. (1951; Carmel, IN: Liberty Fund, Inc., 1997) pg. 409.

94   Charles Dickens, *A Tale of Two Cities* (1859; New York: Barnes & Noble, 2020) pg. 271.

95   David L. Hoffmann, *Stalinist Values: The Cultural Norms of Soviet Modernity 1917-1941* (Ithaca and London: Cornell UP, 2003) pg. 126.

96   R. McNair Wilson, *Monarchy or Money Power* (London: Eyre and Spottiswoode, Ltd., 1933) pg. 72. Quoted in Griffin, pg. 221.

97   Griffin, pgs. 230-3.

98   https://www.biography.com/royalty/louis-xvi.

99   Richard Kelly Hoskins, *War Cycles—Peace Cycles*, 7th printing (Lynchburg: Virginia Publishing Co., 2005) pg. 76.

100   Graham, *Blood Money*, pgs. 44-5.

101   Hoskins, pg. 77.

102   Adams, pgs. 177-87.

103   Leigh, pgs. ix-xviii.

104   Hoskins, pgs. 131-9.

105   Graham, *Blood Money*, pgs. 48-64.

106   Bruce, 1: 431-2.

107   Hannah Arendt, *The Origins of Totalitarianism* (1951; Cleveland and New York: Meridian Books—The World Publishing Co., 2nd enlarged ed., 1958) pg. 322-3.

108   Stanley Burnham, *America's Bimodal Crisis: Black Intelligence in White Society*, 2nd. Ed. (Athens: Foundation for Human Understanding, 1993) pgs. 98-101.

109   Ilana Mercer, *Into the Cannibal's Pot: Lessons for America from Post-Apartheid South Africa* (Seattle: Stairway P, 2011) *passim*.

110   Jose Ortega y Gasset, *Revolt of the Masses*. Trans. Anon. (1930; New York: W. W. Norton & Co., 1993) pgs. 119-21.

111   Rudyard Kipling, "The Gods of the Copybook Headings," (1919). http://www.kiplingsociety.co.uk/poems_copybook.htm.

Sources

Adams, Charles. *When in the Course of Human Events: Arguing the Case for Southern Secession.* Lanham. Boulder. New York. Oxford: Rowman & Littlefield Publishers, Inc., 2000.

Arendt, Hannah. *The Origins of Totalitarianism.* (1951) Cleveland and New York: Meridian Books – The World Publishing Co., second enlarged ed., 1958.

Bennett, Lerone, Jr. *Forced into Glory: Abraham Lincoln's White Dream.* Chicago: Johnson Publishing Co., 2000.

Bowers, Claude. *The Tragic Era: The Revolution after Lincoln.* Cambridge: The Riverside P, 1929.

Boykin, Lt. E. M. *The Falling Flag.* New York: E. J. Hale & Son, 1874.

Bruce, William Cabell. *John Randolph of Roanoke 1773-1833.* 2 vols. New York & London: The Knickerbocker P, 1922.

Burnham, Stanley. *America's Bimodal Crisis: Black Intelligence in White Society*, 2nd ed. Athens: Foundation for Human Understanding, 1993.

Carlyle, Thomas. *The Works of Thomas Carlyle.* 12 vols. Library ed. New York: John B. Alden, 1885.

Chodes, John. *Washington's KKK: The Union League during Southern Reconstruction.* Columbia, S.C.: Shotwell Publishing, 2016.

Churchill, Sir Winston. *A History of the English Speaking Peoples.* 4 vols. New York: Dodd, Meade & Co., 1958.

Dabney, Prof. Robert Lewis, D. D. *A Defense of Virginia (And Through Her, of the South) in the Recent and Pending Contests against the Sectional Party.* New York: E. J. Hale & Son, 1867. Reprinted by Sprinkle Publications, Harrisonburg, VA, 1977.

Dickens, Charles. *A Tale of Two Cities.* (1859) New York: Barnes & Noble, 2020.

DiLorenzo, Thomas J. *The Problem with Lincoln*. Washington, DC: Regnery History, 2020.

—. *The Real Lincoln: A New Look at Abraham Lincoln, His Agenda, and an Unnecessary War*. New York: Three Rivers P, 2003.

Downs, Jim. *Sick from Freedom: African-American Illness and Suffering During the Civil War*. Oxford: Oxford UP, 2012.

DuBois, W. E. B. *The Suppression of the African Slave-Trade to the United States of America 1638-1870*. New York: Longmans, Green & Co., 1896.

Eisenschiml, Otto. *Why Was Lincoln Murdered?* (1937) London: Forgotten Books – Classic Reprint Series, 2018.

Eliot, Charles W., LL D, Ed. *The Harvard Classics*. 50 vols. New York: P. F. Collier & Son, 1910. Vol. 43, *American Historical Documents*.

Faulkner, William. *The Unvanquished*. (1938) New York: Vintage International/Random House, 1991.

Fitzhugh, George. *Cannibals All! or, Slaves Without Masters*. (1857) Cambridge: The Belknap P of Harvard UP, 1960.

Fleming, Walter L., ed. *Documentary History of Reconstruction: Political, Military, Social, Religious, Educational and Industrial, 1865 to 1906*, 2 vols. Cleveland: The Arthur H. Clark Co., 1906.

—. *The Sequel of Appomattox" A Chronicle of the Reunion of the States*. Textbook Ed. The Chronicles of America Series. Ed. Allen Johnson. Gerhard R. Lomer and Charles W. Jeffreys, assistant eds. New Haven: Yale UP, 1919.

Foote, Shelby. *The Civil War: A Narrative*. 3 vols. (1974) New York: Vintage/Random House, 1986.

Graham, John Remington. *Blood Money: The Civil War and the Federal Reserve*. Gretna: Pelican Publishing Co., 2012.

—. *The American Civil War as a Crusade to Free the Slaves*. South Boston, VA: Gerald C. Burnett, M. D., 2016.

Griffin, G. Edward. *The Creature from Jekyll Island: A Second Look at the Federal Reserve*, 4th ed. 1994; Westlake Village, CA: American Media, 2002.

Hoffmann, David L. *Stalinist Values: The Cultural Norms of Soviet Modernity (1917-1941)*. Ithica and London: Cornell UP, 2003.

Hoskins, Richard Kelly. *War Cycles – Peace Cycles*, 7th printing, Lynchburg: Virginia Publishing Co., 2005.

https://www.biography.com/royalty/louis-xvi.

Hurston, Zora Neale. *Barracoon: The Story of the Last "Black Cargo."* Ed. Deborah G. Plant. New York: Amistad/Harper Collins, 2018.

—. *Dust Tracks on a Road: An Autobiography.* 2nd ed. (1942) Urbana: U of Illinois P, 1984.

Journal of the House of Delegates of the State of Virginia for the Extra Session, 1861. Richmond: William F. Ritchie, Public Printer, 1861. Library of Virginia Special Collection.

Kennedy, Paul. *The Rise and Fall of the Great Powers.* New York: Vintage/ Random House, 1989.

Kettell, Thomas Prentice. *Southern Wealth and Northern Profits.* New York: George W. & John A. Wood, 1860.

Kipling, Rudyard. *Rudyard Kipling's Verse.* Inclusive ed. Garden City & New York: Doubleday, Page & Co., 1919.

—. "The Gods of the Copybook Headings," (1919). http://www. kiplingsociety.co.uk/poems_copybook.htm.

Kirk, Russell. *John Randolph of Roanoke: A Study in American Politics,* 4th ed. 1951; Carmel, IN: Liberty Fund, Inc., 1997.

Kizer, Gene, Jr. *Slavery Was Not the Cause of the War Between the States: The Irrefutable Argument.* Charleston and James Island, S.C.: Charleston Athenaeum P, 2014.

Leigh, Philip. *Southern Reconstruction.* Yardley, PA: Westholme Publishing, 2017.

Letcher, Gov. John. Letter to Sec. Simon Cameron, April 16, 1861, in Richmond *Enquirer*, April 18, 1861, pg. 2, col. 1. Microfilm. The Daily Richmond *Enquirer*, Jan. 1, 1861 – June 29, 1861. Film 23, reel 24 (Richmond: Library of Virginia collection).

Mercer, Ilana. *Into the Cannibal's Pot: Lessons for America from Post-Apartheid South Africa.* Seattle: Stairway P, 2011.

Official Records of the Union and Confederate Navies in the War of the Rebellion. 31 vols. Washington, 1894-1927. Ser. 1, Vol. 4.

Orwell, George. *1984.* (1949) New York: Signet Classics/New American Library/Penguin, 1961.

Ortega y Gasset, Jose. *The Revolt of the Masses.* Trans. Anon. (1930) New York: W. W. Norton & Co., 1993.

Pollard, Edward A. *Southern History of the War*. 2 vols. New York: Charles B. Richardson, 1866.

Purnell, Brian and Jeanne Theoharis, eds., with Komozi Woodard. *The Strange Careers of the Jim Crowe North: Segregation and Struggle outside of the South*. New York: New York UP, 2019.

Ramsdell, Charles W. "Lincoln and Fort Sumter." *The Journal of Southern History*, Vol. 3, Issue 3 (August 1937), pgs. 259-88.

Richmond *Enquirer*. Microfilm. The Daily Richmond *Enquirer*, Jan. 1, 1861 – June 29, 1861. Film 23, reel 24. Richmond: Library of Virginia collection.

Semmes, Admiral Raphael, CSN. *Memoirs of Service Afloat During the War Between the States*. (1868) Baton Rouge and London: Louisiana State UP, 1996.

Somers, Robert. *The Southern States since the War 1870-1*. London and New York: MacMillan and Co., 1871.

Tate, Allen. *Collected Poems 1919-1976*. Paperback ed. New York: Farrar Straus Giroux, 2007.

Tennyson, Alfred, Lord. *Idylls of the King*. New York: Airmont Publishing Co., 1969.

Tilley, John Shipley. *Lincoln Takes Command*. Chapel Hill: UNC P, 1941.

de Tocqueville, Alexis. *Democracy in America*. 2 vols. Trans. Henry Reeve. (1835) New York: D. Appleton & Co., 1904. Vol. 1.

Vanden, Harry E. and Gary Prevost. *The Politics of Latin America: The Power Game*. Oxford: Oxford UP, 2002.

Virginia Commission on Constitutional Government. *We the States: An Anthology of Historic Documents and Commentaries thereon, Expounding the State and Federal Relationship*. Richmond: The Wm. Byrd P, 1964.

Virginia History and Government Textbook Commission. *Cavalier Commonwealth: History and Government of Virginia*. New York: McGraw-Hill, 1957.

Virginia Museum of History and Culture: "The Cult of the Lost Cause." https://www.virginiahistory.org/what-you-can-see/story-virginia/ explore-story-virginia/1861-1876/reconstruction.

Von Borcke, Maj. Heros, CSA. *Memoirs of the Confederate War for Independence*. Philadelphia: J. B. Lippincott & Co., 1867.

Waddell, Jos. A. *Annals of Augusta County, Virginia, from 1726 to 1871*. 2nd ed. revised. Staunton: C. Russell Caldwell, 1902.

Wilson, R. McNair. *Monarchy or Money Power*. London: Eyre and Spottiswoode, Ltd. 1933.

Woodson, Dr. Carter G., Ph D. *Free Negro Owners of slaves in the United States in 1830, Together with Absentee Ownership of Slaves in the United States in 1830*. Washington, DC: The Association for the Study of Negro Life and History, 1924.

Acknowledgements

I would like to sincerely thank Dr. Clyde Wilson, Paul Graham, and the staff of Shotwell Publishing for bringing out this revised and updated collection of my essays. In these revolutionary times, it takes courage, which they have in abundance.

I would also like to thank one who is very special to me—and who is a fine writer with book awards to her credit—for providing me with a word processing computer with which to finish this project after my own had given up the ghost. With its familiar program, it has allowed me to put the final touches on the manuscript with ease.

About The Author

A NATIVE OF LYNCHBURG, Virginia, H.V. Traywick, Jr., graduated from the Virginia Military Institute in 1967 with a degree in Civil Engineering and a Regular Commission in the U.S. Army. His service included qualification as an Airborne Ranger and command of an Engineer company in Vietnam where he received the Bronze Star. After his return, he resigned his commission and ended by making a career as a tugboat captain. During this time, he was able to earn a Master of Liberal Arts from the University of Richmond with an international focus on war and cultural revolution. He is a member of The Jamestowne Society, The Society of the Cincinnati in the State of Virginia, and The Sons of Confederate Veterans.

BEST SELLERS AND NEW RELEASES

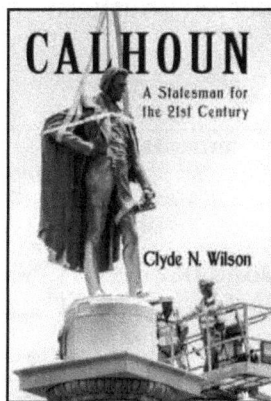

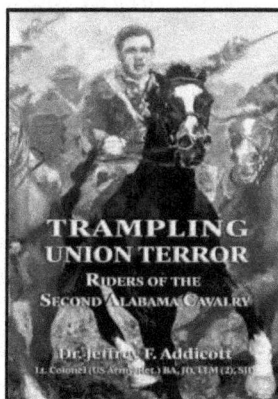

OVER 90 TITLES FOR YOU TO ENJOY

SHOTWELLPUBLISHING.COM

JEFFERY ADDICOTT
Union Terror: Debunking the False Justifications for Union Terror

Trampling Union Terror: Riders of the Second Alabama Cavalry

MARK ATKINS
Women in Combat: Feminism Goes to War

JOYCE BENNETT
Maryland, My Maryland: The Cultural Cleansing of a Small Southern State

GARRY BOWERS
Slavery and The Civil War: What Your History Teacher Didn't Tell You

Dixie Days: Reminiscences Of a Southern Boyhood

The Ultimate Primer for the Southern Outdoorsman

JERRY BREWER
Dismantling the Republic

ANDREW P. CALHOUN
My Own Darling Wife: Letters From A Confederate Volunteer

JOHN CHODES
Segregation: Federal Policy or Racism?

Washington's KKK: The Union League During Southern Reconstruction

WALTER BRIAN CISCO
War Crimes Against Southern Civilians

DAVID T. CRUM
Stonewall Jackson: Saved by Providence

STEPHEN DAVIS
Confederate Triumph: How the South Won Its War for Independence 1861-1863 Volume One:1861

JOHN DEVANNY
Continuities: The South in a Time of Revolution

Lincoln's Continuing Revolution: Essays of M.E. Bradford and Thomas H. Landess

JOSHUA DOGGRELL
Doxed: The Political Lynching of a Southern Cop

JAMES C. EDWARDS
What Really Happened?: Quantrill's Raid On Lawrence, Kansas

TED EHMANN
Boom & Bust In Bone Valley: Florida's Phosphate Mining History 1886-2021

JOHN AVERY EMISON
The Deep State Assassination of Martin Luther King Jr.

DON GORDON
Snowball's Chance: My Kidneys Failed, My Wife Left Me & My Dog Died...

JOHN R. GRAHAM
Constitutional History of Secession

PAUL C. GRAHAM
Confederaphobia

When The Yankees Come: Former Carolina Slaves Remember

Nonsense on Stilts: The Gettysburg Address & Lincoln's Imaginary Nation

JOE D. HAINES
The Diary of Col. John Henry Stover Funk of the Stonewall Brigade, 1861-1862

CHARLES HAYES
The REAL First Thanksgiving

V.P. HUGHES
Col. John Singleton Mosby: In the News 1862-1916

TERRY HULSEY
25 Texas Heroes

The Constitution of Non-State Government: Field Guide to Texas Secession

JOSEPH JAY
Sacred Conviction: The South's Stand for Biblical Authority

JAMES R. KENNEDY
Dixie Rising: Rules For Rebels

Nullifying Federal and State Gun Control: A How-To Guide For Gun Owners

When Rebel Was Cool: Growing Up In Dixie, 1950-1965

Reconstruction: Destroying the Republic and Creating an Empire

Uncle Seth Fought the Yankees: Book 1

WALTER D. KENNEDY
The South's Struggle: America's Hope

Lincoln, The Non-Christian President: Exposing The Myth

Lincoln, Marx, and the GOP

J.R. & W.D. KENNEDY
Jefferson Davis: High Road to Emancipation and Constitutional Government

Yankee Empire: Aggressive Abroad and Despotic at Home

Punished With Poverty: The Suffering South

The South Was Right! 3rd Edition

LEWIS LIBERMAN
Snowflake Buddies; ABC Leftism For Kids!

PHILIP LEIGH
The Devil's Town: Hot Springs During The Gangster Era

U.S. Grant's Failed Presidency

The Causes of the Civil War

The Dreadful Frauds: Critical Race Theory And Identity Politics

JACK MARQUARDT
Around The World In 80 Years: Confessions of a Connecticut Confederate

MICHAEL MARTIN
Southern Grit: Sensing The Siege at Petersburg

SAMUEL MITCHAM
The Greatest Lynching In American History: New York, 1863

Confederate Patton: Richard Taylor and The Red River Campaign

CHARLES T. PACE
Lincoln As He Really Was

Southern Independence. Why War? The War To Prevent Southern Independence

JAMES R. ROESCH
From Founding Fathers To Fire Eaters

KIRKPATRICK SALE
Emancipation Hell: The Tragedy Wrought By Lincoln's Emancipation Proclamation

JOSEPH SCOTCHIE
The Asheville Connection: The Making of a Conservative

Samuel T. Francis and Revolution from the Middle

ANNE W. SMITH
Charlottesville Untold: Inside Unite The Right

Robert E. Lee: A History for Kids

KAREN STOKES
A Legion Of Devils: Sherman In South Carolina

*The Burning of Columbia, S.C.: A Review
of Northern Assertions and Southern Facts*

Carolina Love Letters

*Fortunes of War:
The Adventures of a German Confederate*

*A Confederate in Paris:
Letters of A. Dudley Mann 1867-1879*

Bessie in Love and War

JOSEPH R. STROMBERG
*Southern Story and Song:
Country Music in the 20th Century*

JACK TROTTER
Last Train to Dixie

JOHN THEURSAM
Key West's Civil War

H.V. TRAYWICK, JR.
*Along The Shadow Line:
A Road Trip through History and Memory
on the Old Confederate Border*

LESLIE TUCKER
*Old Times There Should Not Be Forgotten:
Cultural Genocide In Dixie*

JOHN VINSON
Southerner Take Your Stand!

MARK R. WINCHELL
*Confessions of a Copperhead:
Culture and Politics in the Modern South*

CLYDE N. WILSON
Calhoun: A Statesman for the 21st Century

*Lies My Teacher Told Me: The True History
of the War For Southern Independence*

The Yankee Problem: An American Dilemma

*Annals Of The Stupid Party:
Republicans Before Trump*

*Nullification:
Reclaiming The Consent of the Governed*

The Old South: 50 Essential Books

The War Between The States: 60 Essential Books

*Reconstruction and the New South,
1865-1913: 50 Essential Books*

*The South 20th Century And Beyond:
50 Essential Books*

*Southern Poets and Poems, 1606-1860:
The Land They Loved, Volume 1*

*Confederate Poets and Poems, Vol1
The Land They Loved, Volume II*

Looking For Mr. Jefferson

African American Slavery in Historical Perspective

JOE WOLVERTON
*What Degree Of Madness?: Madison's Method
To Make American States Again*

WALTER KIRK WOOD
*Beyond Slavery: The Northern Romantic
Nationalist Origins of America's Civil War*

SHOTWELLPUBLISHING.COM

Green Altar (Literary Imprint)

CATHARINE SAVAGE BROSMAN
*An Aesthetic Education
and Other Stories (2nd Ed)*

Chained Tree, Chained Owls: Poems

Aerosols and Other Poems

Partial Memoirs

RANDALL IVEY
*A New England Romance:
and Other Southern Stories*

The Gift of Gab

SUZANNE JOHNSON
Maxcy Gregg's Sporting Journals 1842-1858

JAMES E. KIBLER, JR.
Tiller : Claybank County Series, Vol. 4

The Gentler Gamester

*Beyond The Stone: Poems of Tribute
& Remembrance*

THOMAS MOORE
*A Fatal Mercy:
The Man Who Lost The Civil War*

PERRIN LOVETT
The Substitute, Tom Ironsides 1

Judging Athena

KAREN STOKES
Belles

Carolina Twilight

Honor in the Dust

The Immortals

The Soldier's Ghost: A Tale of Charleston

WILLIAM THOMAS
*Runaway Haley:
An Imagined Family Saga*

*The Field of Justice: Moonshine
and Murder in North Georgia*

CLYDE N. WILSON
*Southern Poets and Poems, 1606-1860:
The Land They Loved, Volume 1*

*Confederate Poets and Poems, Vol1
The Land They Loved, Volume II*

Gold-Bug
(Mystery & Suspense Imprint)

BRANDI PERRY
Splintered: A New Orleans Tale

MARTIN WILSON
To Jekyll and Hide

www.ingramcontent.com/pod-product-compliance
Lightning Source LLC
Chambersburg PA
CBHW072147090426
42739CB00013B/3308